What Would You Die For?

Perpetua's Passion

What Would You Die For?

Perpetua's Passion

Translation and Notes by
Caitlin A. Allender
Mary Costantino
Richard Gibbons
Irene A. Murphy
Kimberly Sanders
Lauren A. Teresa
Elizabeth C. Waters
Nathan E. Zawie

Edited and with an introduction by
Joseph J. Walsh

apprentice
house

Baltimore, Maryland
www.apprenticehouse.com

Project managers: Katharine Dailey and
Dana Susan Kirkpatrick

Cover design by Alexis Turro
Back cover art by Cynthia Von Buhler

First printing
10 9 8 7 6 5 4 3 2 1

ISBN: 978-1-934074-02-2

apprentice
house

Baltimore, Maryland
www.apprenticehouse.com

Aperio Series: Loyola Humane Texts

Through "Aperio Series: Loyola Humane Texts," Loyola College in Maryland publishes important and illuminating texts in the Humanities that have been edited, annotated, and/or translated by the College's students in collaboration with faculty. Students also work with faculty to design and publish the texts. The texts are intended for all readers but should be of particular interest and use to college students and in undergraduate classes.

Contents

Acknowledgments

■

Our thanks to the Center for the Humanities at Loyola College, the Loyola College Humanities Symposium, and the Department of Classics for their financial and moral support. Angela Christman, Stephen Fowl, Gayla McGlamery, James Rives, Frank Romer, and Martha Taylor were kind enough to look at the Introduction and improve it considerably. They are, of course, not in the least responsible for the shortcomings of style and substance that remain. The Interlibrary Loan office at the Loyola-Notre Dame Library did its usual exceptional job of finding everything we needed quickly.

Special thanks to David Haddad, Patty Ingram and Dan Schlapbach for their support of this project, to Treasa Beyer for proof-reading the text, and especially to Martha Taylor, whose faith in this project made this book possible.

The art on the back cover is a detail of the illustration commissioned as part of the design for the 2006 Humanities Symposium entitled: "What Would you Die For? Perpetua's Passion." The illustration was art directed by Laura Franek and created by Cynthia Von Buhler. The materials used to create the illustration are gouache on linen canvas with wood, plaster, gold leaf, and a real feather pen. The original artwork was then photographed using a medium format camera.

A Word on References
In the Text

■

In this volume, passages in <u>Perpetua's Passion</u> are cross-referenced by section numbers (such as 1.3), not by page numbers. This will make it easier to find spots in the text but also to identify the Latin corresponding to the translation; section 3.2 in the English, then, is a translation of 3.2 in the Latin. The original Latin is provided in Appendix 1.

Works of modern scholarship cited more than once are referred to by the author's last name with a word from the work's title; Rives, "Piety," for example, refers to Rives, James, "The Piety of a Persecutor," <u>Journal of Early Christian Studies</u> 4.1 (1996) 1-26. The full citations for these texts and articles are in the "Recommended Reading" section of this text.

Preface

The great secret of morals is Love; or an identification
of ourselves with the beautiful which exists in thought,
action, or person, not our own. A man, to be greatly
good, must imagine intensely and comprehensively;
he must put himself in the place of another and of
many others; the pains and pleasure of his species must
become his own. The great instrument of moral good is
the imagination; and poetry administers to the effect by
acting upon the cause.
  – Percy Bysshe Shelley, "A Defense of Poetry" (1821)

This new translation has a twofold agenda. First, we
hope to encourage twenty-first-century readers to become
acquainted with a group of martyrs through the martyrs'
own words and to understand both how they came to find
themselves in a harrowing and ultimately fatal predicament
and why they responded to this situation in the remarkable
way they did. <u>Perpetua's Passion</u> is an important historical
document, providing an extraordinary window through
which to view and understand the past.

Our second hope is that this work will help readers consider important issues about their own lives. Just as, according to Shelley, poetry helps expand the moral imagination,
so too can history expand our imaginative sympathies by

offering the stories of other lives, stories that may speak to us with particular power and credibility because they are the stories of real people. When people of the past speak with their own voices and reflect on their own experience, as Perpetua and her fellow martyr Saturus do in this text, the reader's experience is all the more intense. And so the hope is that through this translation Perpetua's "pains and pleasure" will strengthen readers' moral imaginations and so provoke serious, even uncomfortable, self-examination. The goal of heightening our sympathy is not, of course, to have us weep more readily when we read or hear of others' suffering; rather it is to have us ask what we owe to those around us, what we should make of our own lives, and what we value most. Our answers to such questions can change who we are and how we walk in the world.

Introduction

Here I stand. I cannot do otherwise. God help me! Amen.

– Martin Luther[1]

What would you die for?

Ours is a world of extremes. As twenty-first century terrorism has taught us, there is no shortage of people who are willing to die and even kill for their beliefs. At the other end of the spectrum are those who find very little worth taking a stand for, let alone dying for. It is not uncommon in America today to find on campuses students who are confident that they would put their lives on the line for their families (and perhaps for their closest friends), but who will admit that they cannot find anything else – belief, conviction, principle, place, cause, or institution – for which they would be willing to die.

<u>Perpetua's Passion</u> tells the story of a young woman and her friends who found something worth dying for. It would

---

[1] "Hier stehe ich. Ich kann nicht anders. Gott helfe mir. Amen." From Luther's 18 April 1521 speech at the Diet of Worms; the Diet wound up declaring his ideas heretical.

have been easy for them to evade death; all they had to do to save their lives was deny their identity as Christians and make a token pagan sacrifice for the emperor's welfare. Mere words and hollow formalities. The death they were to suffer was painful, terrifying, and humiliatingly public – they were to be mauled to death by animals in front of a large and raucous crowd. And before their execution, they endured days of imprisonment, time aplenty to ponder the horrors that awaited them, to grow apprehensive, and to doubt. Yet they persevered and bore their gruesome deaths when the time came.

Some students I have taught have found Perpetua and her friends a bit too eager to martyr themselves. They acknowledge Perpetua's courage but consider her a fanatic, someone they not only would not emulate, but someone whose actions they find somewhat absurd, but nonetheless unsettling. Perhaps Perpetua is a bit too hot for a culture that prizes cool. A few students have noted the similarities between these early Christian martyrs and twenty-first century Islamist suicide bombers: their willingness to endure death, their religious conviction, their unswerving and unquestioning certainty, their youth,[2] their refusal to compromise, their disdain for this world, and wild optimism about the next. Indeed, these similarities are noteworthy. Speaking on the eve of an "operation," one Palestinian suicide terrorist described his feelings as follows:

> On the night before an operation, we had that feeling when you first get married, on the night of the wedding, so excited…That feeling comes from the fact that soon you will see the Gardens of Heaven; you will see the

---

[2] Perpetua was around twenty-two, and the text seems to suggest that the other martyrs were probably young as well (see Harris & Gifford, <u>Acts</u> 5).

Prophet and your friends who died before. We were so excited, and were full of happiness. In that moment, we lived a sort of higher faith. It's a feeling like you are in the sky, and the earthly world gets smaller and smaller and smaller. This feeling gives you all the happiness.[3]

Substitute "martyrdom" for "operation" and "Jesus" for "the Prophet," and you could imagine Perpetua making this statement. The differences, however, are just as striking. Early Christian martyrs did not kill, not even themselves, as modern suicide bombers do, nor did they call their non-Christian neighbors and adversaries "sons of monkeys and pigs," as Islamist radicals sometimes refer to Jews. Perhaps the most telling difference is the absence of the humiliation, hatred, and rage that fuel so much modern terrorism – Islamic, Christian, and Jewish alike. Nor were ethnic pride and nationalist aspirations part of the ancient mix.

When Americans of the twenty-first century look beyond our borders, we fear that fanaticism is thriving. When we look about our own communities, however, we may see a dearth of conviction and passion that is almost as disconcerting. Most of us in our mundane, unexciting lives are not confronted with the question, "What would you die for?" But the story of Perpetua and her friends suggests that behind this question lurks another one: "What are you living for?"

What Is a Passion?

The Apostle urges us to share in the remembrances of the saints, fully aware that to call to mind those who have

---

[3] Oliver, Anne Marie, & Steinberg, Paul F., The Road to Martyr's Square (Oxford U. Press, 2005) 136.

passed their lives in the faith wisely with all their hearts gives strength to those who are striving to imitate the better things. Indeed, more fitting is it that we should remember the martyr Pionius seeing that this apostolic man, being one of us, kept many from straying while he dwelt in the world, and when he was finally called to the Lord and bore witness, he left us this writing for our instruction that we might have it even to this day as a memorial of his teaching.

– <u>Passion of Pionius</u> 1[4]

<u>The Passion of Perpetua</u> is the account of the arrest, trial, imprisonment, and execution of a small group of Christian martyrs in Carthage, the capital of the Roman province of Africa. A series of such accounts survive from the Roman Empire, and they are known variously as <u>Passions</u>, <u>Acts</u>, and <u>Martyrdoms</u>. [5] The basic story of these accounts is essentially the same – arrest, trial, execution – but they can differ widely in presentation. The formula, boy meets girl, boy loses girl, boy wins girl, has generated thousands of books, movies, plays, and television shows, but variations in the plotting, characterization, detail, and language allow for tremendous variety. As with love stories, so too with martyr accounts.[6] <u>The Passion of the Scillitan Martyrs</u>[7] – of particular interest to us since these martyrs,

---

[4] This is Musurillo's translation.

[5] <u>Passions</u>="sufferings," from the Latin *passio*; <u>Acts</u>="deeds" or even "accomplishments," from the Latin *acta* (though the word here does not designate the acts of a play, the ancient accounts frequently have theatrical elements and even, at times, in their presentation of dialogue resemble the script of a play or movie); <u>Martyrdoms</u>=martyrdoms, from the Greek *marturion* (the basic and original idea behind the word was "bearing witness").

[6] On the variety of the accounts of martyrdoms, see Musurillo, <u>Acts</u> xi-lvii, and Gary A. Bisbee, <u>Pre-Decian Acts of Martyrs and Commentarii</u> (Fortress Press, 1988). The best way to get a sense of their variety, however, is to read the translations of the actual accounts in Musurillo.

[7] Named after their hometown in Africa. The town has not yet been identified, nor do we even know its name (Scillium, perhaps).

like Perpetua, were tried and executed in Carthage – reads like a court transcript. The entire text is but two pages long in most editions, and the report of the trial's conclusion and execution of the martyrs is as short and spare as a TV crawl line story:

> The governor Saturninus ordered that a herald pro-
>   claim the following:
> "I have ordered the execution of Speratus, Nartzalus,
>   Cittinus, Veturius, Felix, Aquilinus, Laetantius,
>   Januaria, Generosa, Vestia, Donata, and Secunda."
> They all said together:
> "Thanks be to God."
> And at once they were beheaded for the name of
>   Christ. (16-17)[8]

The Passion of Pionius, in contrast, is over fifteen pages long, and in it the martyr gets to deliver two speeches that are each longer than the entire Scillitan Passion.

The ancient Greeks and Romans believed that great deeds should be recorded. In the fifth century BCE, Herodotus states this explicitly in the opening sentence of his History:

> This is the publication of the research of Herodotus of Halicarnassus, written in order that what humankind has done will not be forgotten over time, and so that great and remarkable deeds, some brought before the world by Greeks, some by foreigners, may have their glory; besides all this, why they fought against each other.
>
> – History 1.1

---

[8] The full Latin text with a new English translation of the The Passion of the Scillitan Martyrs is provided in Appendix 2.

The quotation from the <u>Passion of Pionius</u> that introduces this section makes perfectly clear that early Christians shared this idea, though for them greatness that should be recorded lay not in military or political success but in living wisely and uncompromisingly in the faith, even unto death.

And so, <u>Passions</u> present themselves as history, as records of what actually happened. Their agenda, however, was more complex. In early Christian liturgy, recollection of Jesus' sufferings, death, and resurrection was more than a revisiting of the historical record, no matter how important; it represented "a living sacrifice offered up to God in the present."[9] When martyr accounts were read to Christian congregations, these too became part of the believers' own immediate experience. The quotation from the <u>Passion of Pionius</u> also demonstrates that the accounts of the martyrs primarily aimed to inspire other Christians to show similar faith and courage should they be confronted with the choice between faithfulness and saving their lives, to provide, as one <u>Passion</u> puts it, "training and preparation" for future martyrs.[10] The martyrs' great sacrifice, moreover, should inspire Christians to lead more pious lives in the mundane day-to-day. Their steadfastness could be held up as worthy of emulation when lesser temptations – dishonesty, sexual impurity, selfishness – threatened. They would strengthen every Christian "to imitate better things." Authors, redactors, and revisers of <u>Passions</u> have also used them to provide theological instruction and to comment on contemporary theological concerns.

---

[9] Robert Wilken, <u>The Spirit of Early Christian Thought. Seeking the Face of God</u> (Yale University Press, 2003) 35; for a discussion of the early Christian notion of remembrance, see Wilken, pp. 32-35.

[10] <u>Martyrdom of Polycarp</u> 18.

It seems clear that piety inspired some ancient redactors and editors to enhance the accounts they received, to make them more dramatic, more heroic, more inspiring – but less historical. Modern readers and scholars consequently doubt the accuracy and even the authenticity of some of them. Edward Gibbon, the great eighteenth-century historian of the Roman Empire (and a more effective adversary of early Christianity than its Roman persecutors) cleverly, unkindly, and perhaps somewhat insightfully, suggests, "The monks of succeeding ages, who, in their peaceful solitudes, entertained themselves with diversifying the deaths and sufferings of primitive martyrs, have frequently invented torments of a much more refined and ingenious nature."[11] To test the reliability of Passions, scholars look for inconsistencies in surviving versions of martyrdoms, errors of fact, and implausible melodrama. In contrast, evidence that the surviving text was composed very close to the time of the events it recounts lends credibility. The lean, apparently unembellished text of the Scillitan martyrs, to give an example, argues for its authenticity, although a brief portion of the account appears to be missing. [12]

The Passion of Perpetua, despite its dream visions and considerable drama, is almost universally considered to be authentic. About half of the Passion is autobiographical; the other half is reported by an eyewitness to many of its events.[13] The first two sections are the eyewitness/editor's introduction; sections 3-10 present Perpetua's experience

---

[11] The Decline and Fall of the Roman Empire (ed. Hans-Friedrich Mueller; The Modern Library, 2003; originally 1776) 285. This is typical of Gibbon's sentiments, although here he is commenting on the lurid elements in some Passions.

[12] Some modern readers find the leaner texts (like the Scillitan) more moving; less can be more.

[13] At the very least, a local contemporary of the martyrdom.

of events in prison and at trial in her own words, including detailed accounts of dreams; after a brief transition, the ancient editor provides Saturus' account of his own vision in sections 11-13; for the remainder of the <u>Passion</u> (14-21), the editor takes over as author/witness, since the martyrs were in no position to record their own deaths.

There is little doubt that the sections attributed to Perpetua and Saturus were actually written by them and that the editor/co-author was their contemporary and most likely present at their deaths.[14] However, not all readers accept the martyrs' representations of their visions and behavior as perfectly historical. Did Perpetua actually dream what she claimed she dreamed? Did she have dreams along the lines described but that she greatly (and perhaps unconsciously) embellished after waking?[15] Did she make the dreams up? We cannot know. But it is clear that Perpetua and Saturus

---

[14] For skepticism concerning Saturus' account, however, see note to section 11.1 of the text. I do not find the skeptics' reservations persuasive.

[15] We should also keep in mind that Perpetua was writing in a culture that allowed historians and biographers greater latitude in embroidering their accounts. Greek and Roman historians typically composed speeches and then put them in the mouths of historical personages, often without regard for the words actually spoken or even whether there was evidence that a speech had been given at all. Readers did not think of these speeches as transcripts of what was actually said but rather as historians' attempts to delineate the speakers' characters and to explain the significance of the events narrated. And these speeches were expected to be a good read. An ancient historian who inserted a genuine but drab speech into his account would incur ridicule, for historians were judged as much on their literary style as on their content. The best ancient biographers focused on revealing the character of their subjects, and they intended that their works first and foremost give readers examples of virtue to emulate and vice to avoid. The greatest of ancient biographers, Plutarch, for example, often frustrates historians by rushing past major events and dwelling on seemingly insignificant and even apocryphal incidents. This is because these historically insignificant incidents may do a better job than great events of teaching us about the hero and ourselves. Although she neither was nor claimed to be an historian, it is not out of the question that this mentality influenced Perpetua's depiction of her dreams. In the ancient Christian community, however, most believers would have assumed that she had dreamed precisely what she described.

were quite conscious of the fact that their sacrifice provided a powerful encouragement to others to persevere in their faith, that they themselves were exemplars, what we would call role models. Their actions were intended, in significant part, then, to encourage others to do the right thing, and the text they helped create was meant to serve the same function. Everything they did, said, and wrote was carried out with the impact on other believers[16] very much in mind. In a sense, the way Perpetua, Saturus, and their friends ended their lives and the text they composed to commemorate that end are in purpose one and the same. And through this commemoration, they hoped to be part of the spiritual lives of future generations of Christians; the ancient editor of Perpetua's Passion asserts that those who read or hear this text will "have fellowship with the holy martyrs" (1).[17] Did this consciousness induce embellishment and thus give us a richer Passion, but a less historically accurate one? Or did it inspire the protagonists to exceptional and authentic deeds worthy of remembrance, of a prized place in the historical record? Readers must decide for themselves.

The Life of a Roman Woman

> The Christians have recruited from the lowest dregs of society and women too, since they naturally tend to be credulous and flighty...
>
> – Minucius Felix, Octavius 8

---

[16] And potential converts as well.

[17] And in fact later Christians did enjoy in their liturgy a kind of fellowship with the martyrs: in African churches, a version of their martyrdom would be read to the congregation on their feast day. Some of the sermons accompanying these liturgical readings have survived; for a translation of four by Augustine, for example, see W. H. Shewring, Four Spiritual Classics (Sheed and Ward, 1931) 45-59.

The ancient Greeks are notorious for their misogyny. In his catalogue of female types, the poet Semonides, for example, identified women with sows, vixens, asses, ferrets, haughty mares, and monkeys. The only commendable type of woman is likened to a bee, and it is easy to figure out what it is about the bee-woman that pleased Semonides. At most times and in most places in ancient Greece, women's actual lives were little better than their reputation. They endured seclusion (in respectable households respectable women were confined to the home and strictly to private rooms when men visited) and exclusion (women played virtually no role in the political and public lives of their states). No repute was better than ill repute, but better than a good reputation as well, as the Greek historian Thucydides famously has Pericles say in his great funeral oration for Athens' war dead:

> Since I am obliged to say something of feminine virtue, I will express the whole thing to you who are widows in this brief recommendation: your glory will be great if you are no worse than nature has made your sex, and if there is as little talk as possible about you, whether the talk concerns your excellence or it is a reproach.
> – <u>Peloponnesian War</u> 3.45

Pericles neglects to mention how you can have great glory when nothing is known of you.

One can certainly find statements of Roman misogyny as well – Juvenal's sixth satire comes to mind, although Juvenal seems not to have approved of many men either. It would be more accurate, however, to view the attitude of Roman men as paternalistic rather than misogynistic. A passage from the jurist Ulpian, who belonged to the generation immediately after Perpetua's, captures the attitude perfectly:

> Guardians are appointed for both males and females; for males before puberty because of the weakness of their youth; for females, however, both before and after puberty because of the weakness of their sex and their ignorance of legal matters.
>
> — <u>Rules</u> 11.1

Someone needs to keep an eye out for (and on) women and children, since obviously neither can take care of themselves. Unlike Greek women, Roman women joined their husbands at dinner parties and had more freedom of association and of movement in public, but as "the weaker sex" they too were for the most part excluded from politics, war, and law, the principal paths to authority, leadership, and greatness in Roman society. [18] Only by serving the interests of her husband could a Roman woman attain excellence. For instance, Pliny gushes about the achievements of his beloved wife, but they are all in his service:

> My wife is extremely sharp and extremely frugal, and she loves me, an indication of her fidelity. On top of this, her affection for me has induced in her an interest in literature. She has my books, can't put them down, and even memorizes them. How concerned she is, when I am going to plead in court! How delighted she is when I have completed the task! She assigns messengers to the

---

[18] We might add business as well. By providing an opportunity to acquire wealth, virtually a prerequisite to authority and leadership, business could help pave the path to greatness. In the Roman Empire, however, it was much more difficult to make a fortune through business than it is today. If you were one of the very lucky few to strike it rich, moreover, it would probably take a generation or two to translate your money into social and political prominence.

court to report to her the reaction to my speech, any applause I garner, and the outcome of the case. And if I am giving a public lecture, she sits nearby, concealed behind a curtain, and eagerly laps up any praise I win. She even sets my poetry to the lyre and sings it. No instructor has taught her how to do this, only love, the very best teacher.

— <u>Letters</u> 4.19

If Pliny's wife desired to shine in public life and in the arts, she had to do it vicariously through her husband. A talented, aspiring Roman woman, then, had to fulfill her ambitions in the roles of wife and mother. Unlike Thucydides' perfect little invisible Greek woman, however, a Roman woman could win glory through extraordinary character or deeds in the domestic sphere. Pliny, again, provides an example. The Emperor Claudius had given a certain Caecina Paetus no choice but to commit suicide, and he was having a difficult time bringing himself to do to it. His wife Arria showed greater courage, guiding her husband to the inevitable:

Her most glorious deed, surely, was to draw a sword, plunge it into her heart, then pull it out and offer it to her husband, saying these immortal, even divine, words: "Paetus, it does not hurt."

— <u>Letters</u> 3.16

And what, according to Pliny, forged Arria's steely resolve? A desire all Romans, man and woman, would understand perfectly: "But still she had before her eyes, as she was acting and speaking thus, the hope of fame and immortality." Arria was aiming high, and she hit the mark.

For all their exclusion from public life, Roman women, particularly of the upper classes, not infrequently showed themselves to be a feisty lot whose ambitions went beyond the home. Arria's deeds may have been confined within the household and her relation to her husband, but the fame she won shone in the broader world. Women of the imperial household constantly tried to exert influence and wield political power through their husbands and sons. Sometimes they even wielded it directly. In his biography of Rome's second emperor, Tiberius, Suetonius recounts how Tiberius became irritated with the political involvement and clout of his formidable mother Livia (also wife of the first and greatest emperor, Augustus):

> But he often warned her to stay out of important business that was inappropriate for a woman, especially when he heard that she had been on the spot at a fire near the temple of Vesta, pushing the people and the soldiers to help out more vigorously. This is the sort of thing she did when her husband was alive.
>
> – Tiberius 50

The most influential of all empresses was Julia Domna, the wife of Septimius Severus, the African emperor in whose reign Perpetua and her friends were martyred. Julia was Septimius' most trusted political advisor, and she accompanied him on many of his official travels and even military campaigns, which garnered her the title, "Mother of the Military Camp." Septimius seems to have been happy to have his formidable wife perceived as his helpmate in office, and she was. Perpetua may well have seen Julia, and indications of her authority, when the imperial family made a lengthy and sensational tour of Africa. Did Julia's prominence make an impression on Perpetua? We can only speculate, since her jail diary indicates that she had more pressing things on her mind.

Of course, life and aspirations were different for the great mass of women of the Roman Empire. Like their lower-class fathers, sons, and husbands, they were poor and had little prospect of attaining power, influence, or glory. Many of them worked, as their families struggled to make ends meet. This brought greater involvement in the world beyond the home and probably greater freedom, too, but not leadership or prestige. Roman society's upper classes, like aristocrats throughout most of human history, despised work, at least in the sense of earning a living through labor. And Perpetua was clearly a gentlewoman – the <u>Passion</u> characterizes her as "of a highly respectable family and...also liberally educated."[19] For her, the paths twenty-first century women tread to authority and respect – business, politics, public service, the arts[20] – were blocked.

Around 200 CE, the situation of Christian women in the Roman Empire was, in most respects, not much different from that of pagan women. The extent to which early Christian women occupied positions of leadership in their church communities is hotly debated. And no wonder. Interpretation of the ancient evidence plays a significant role in modern denominational decisions about the leadership roles women play in Christian congregations today. Those who maintain that early Christian women were full participants in all levels of Christian worship and life argue that eventually ancient male writers imposed an androcentric narrative on an egalitarian early Christian experience and reality; according to this view, modern opponents of women clergy misread and distort the early evidence to

---

[19] *honeste nata, liberaliter instituta* (2).

[20] In many societies, entertainers have lived outside the bounds of respectability. This was certainly true of ancient Rome, where many performers were slaves or former slaves.

preserve this exclusion of women from prominence in the Church.[21]   One of the ancient culprits would be Perpetua's fellow African Tertullian, who rails against women assuming positions of authority in their congregations: "These heretical women – how impudent they are! They have the audacity to teach, to debate, to perform exorcisms, to cure, perhaps even to baptize!"[22] Tertullian's ire may represent his era's most common (male, at any rate) view of women performing important functions in the Church, but his comments also reveal that at least some women in Perpetua's day were in fact performing these functions and that

---

[21] Representative of this view is Elizabeth Schüssler Fiorenza, "'You are not to be called Father.' Early Christian History in a Feminist Perspective," Cross Currents 29.3 (1979) 301-23, with bibliography. See, too Schüssler Fiorenza's lengthier treatment, In Memory of Her. A Feminist Theological Reconstruction of Christian Origins (Crossroad, 1983/1992), although this is primarily a discussion of the New Testament.

[22] From his essay attacking heretics, On the Prescription of Heretics (de praescriptione 41.5). Since we will be running into Tertullian again and again, it will be useful to know a bit about him. He was an important and prolific Christian writer who commented, usually with considerable passion, on a great many theological, moral, and social issues of his day. He began as an orthodox Christian, but he evolved into a Montanist ("orthodox" here does not indicate any connection, historical or otherwise, to modern Orthodox confessions; it means, rather, that for the most part he shared the views of mainstream Christianity and its hierarchy of that day). Montanism was a second- and third-century Christian movement (some would say heresy; the people commonly referred to today as Montanists, however, regarded themselves as the strictest and most authentic Christians) that emphasized the uncompromising embrace of martyrdom and the authenticity and authority of prophecy in their own post-biblical age. His writings are particularly helpful in understanding Perpetua's story, since as a fellow African, Christian, and contemporary, he sheds more light than any other source on her cultural and religious environment and situation. His many writings on martyrdom, composed in the same place and during the same period of time in which Perptua and her friends were martyred, are uniquely valuable in explaining the martyrs' mindset and that of their neighbors – pagan as well as Christian. Perpetua's Passion, moreover, exhibits unambiguous Montanist inclinations in respect both to martyrdom and to prophecy; indeed, Tertullian has been proposed as the author of the sections of the Passion that Perpetua and Saturus did not compose.

such female presumption was worth attacking.[23] Perpetua attained eminence in her congregations, then, at a time when Christians were aware of this possibility and yet when women's prominence was under assault.[24]

Perpetua's description of her feelings, actions, and visions is unique, and not just because it provides an unparalleled personal view of a Roman Christian woman's experience unfiltered and undistorted by male voices.[25] In many ways, Perpetua challenges and inverts Roman expectations of her gender; indeed, she puts into question its

---

[23] That Tertullian considered these women heretics is not an issue for this volume, and I am neither competent to assess nor interested in assessing the orthodoxy or heresy of any ancient person. For the purposes of this text, anyone who considered him or herself Christian will be regarded as a Christian. We should remember that early Christianity was riven by disagreements of many sorts, and some Christians employed fiercer rhetoric against their theological adversaries than against their pagan persecutors. Tertullian's case is revealing. In his writings, he mercilessly attacked those he considered heretics; ironically, due to his late Montanism (or Montanist tendencies), he himself wound up considered a heretic or, at least, to have flirted with heresy.

[24] For an examination of the frustrating dynamics of Christianity's message of freedom for women and the Church's subsequent restriction of that freedom, see Jouette Bassler, "The Widow's Tale: A Fresh Look at 1 Tim 5:3-16," Journal of Biblical Literature 103.1 (1984) 23-41.

[25] The editor and other early Christian writers (including St. Augustine) have garnered criticism for trying to determine the reader's reaction to and understanding of Perpetua's words (see, among others, Shaw, "Perpetua" 33-45, and Salisbury, Passion 166-179), and they have been accused of trying to suppress or rewrite the aspects of her voice that discomfort male presumptions of primacy and authority. Regardless of these writers' intentions and the efficacy of their efforts, we nonetheless have Perpetua's own words, an exceptional circumstance. (Shaw, in a fair-minded observation towards the end of his essay, confesses that he and other modern commentators are essentially doing the same thing as the early Christian commentators he criticizes ["Perpetua" 45].) Perpetua's section of the Passion is the earliest surviving writing by a Christian woman; personal reflections in prose of ancient woman, pagan or Christian, are extremely rare. Of the thousands of ancient writers whose names we know, only about one hundred are women's, and of those the writings of only about half have survived. Most of what has survived is fragmentary and in poetic form – and thus, however personal, consciously literary. For translations of these fragments, see I. M. Plant, Women Writers of Ancient Greece and Rome (University of Oklahoma Press, 2004); see pages 1-9 on the rarity and nature of extant writings by ancient women.

very essence. A respectable Roman woman's life was, as we have seen, defined, understood, and judged by her diligence and faithfulness within the household. Even the assertive empress Julia Domna derived her political power and authority from her husband and his wishes. If we keep this in mind, Perpetua's choices and her own sense of them were downright subversive: despite her anguish about her infant son – again and again she expresses concern for him – she gives the child up; her father, who ought to have authority and power over her, is reduced to throwing himself at her feet in supplication and acknowledging her as his master, *Domina* ("Lady"), the Latin word whose masculine form is employed in this and other Christian texts to refer to the Lord, God; the other figure who should be reining her in, her husband, is completely absent from the text;[26] she designates as brother and sister people who are not part of her family; she is assertive in the face of male authority outside the home; and so on. She has, essentially, rejected her role, her very identity as a Roman woman, and relocated herself within a new, entirely different sort of family. And this relocation – dislocation, from the Roman point of view – is so radical, so devoid of traditional points of reference, that in one of her visions she becomes a man and fights, and yet the pronouns that refer to this Perpetua-man are feminine. This vision reminds us of Paul's famous assertion. "There is neither Jew nor Greek, there is neither slave nor free, there is neither male nor female; for you are all one in Christ Jesus" (Gal 3:28), and yet one wonders what else is pondered,

---

[26] One might be inclined to see Perpetua as typical of a pattern in ancient literature and myth: dsfunctional families characterized by strong women usurping masculine behavior and speech from weak men; in the Passion, Perpetua's father plays this role. The unexplained absence of her husband, however, complicates the pattern.

questioned, or suggested by Perpetua's transformation.[27]

Perpetua's faith required that she take radical steps, but her liberation from society's norms and constraints brought benefits as well. Her steadfastness presented her with an opportunity for leadership and authority that the Roman institutions and values in which she had grown up denied her and that the direction of the Christian organization and faith that she adopted was moving to forbid her. One of the most remarkable features of Perpetua's story is the unambiguous and undeniable prestige and deference that her steadfast courage won for her.[28] Whether on some level this opportunity helped motivate her is for readers to decide for themselves. What is undeniable, however, are the effects of her choice: authority among and respect from her contemporaries, admiration and awe among succeeding generations, whatever their faith.

---

[27] In The Male Woman. A Feminine Ideal in the Early Church (Acta Universitatis Upsaliensis; Almqvist & Wiksell International, 1990; the text is edited by René Kieffer, since Professor Aspegren died before she could complete the book), Kerstin Aspegren analyzes the tendency in ancient pagan and Christian texts (almost all authored by men) to characterize exceptional women as masculine; her analysis of Perpetua's Passion demonstrates how Perpetua fits the pattern but also emphasizes how she transcends it (133-143).

[28] Since this enhanced position was also a path to death, its duration was limited. We do not know how long Perpetua and the other martyrs were held in jail, but prisoners could be held in Roman jails for quite a long time. Had she suffered persecution but survived, she would have been a confessor, that is, a Christian who had proved her or his faithfulness in the face of pain and danger but had lived. Confessors, too, enjoyed considerable prestige in the Church, not to mention longer lives, but it is very doubtful that Perpetua's story and her reflections on it would have attained their prized position or even survived had she not been martyred.

Setting

> Only Rome surpasses Carthage in wealth, population,
> and size, as the African city competes with Alexandria in
> Egypt to be the second city of the Empire.
>
> – Herodian[29]

Perpetua's story takes place in the Roman Empire in
203 CE. The Empire is one of the most curious and successful political institutions in human history; its nature was
largely determined by the centrifugal and centripetal forces,
the push and pull of a centrally governed but politically and
ethnically diverse institution, that made the Empire simultaneously one and many. We might view it as a vast checkerboard, a single object divided into many distinct pieces.
Holding it together, ultimately, was Rome's military, but the
army alone did not suffice to make it work so well and last so
long. Over several centuries, millions of people, Roman and
provincial alike, led relatively normal lives simultaneously as
participants in local communities and as either subjects or
citizens of the Empire. This is a remarkable fact, considering that the Empire encompassed the entire Mediterranean
world, conjoined parts of three continents, and at times
reached as far as Scotland in the northwest and the Fertile
Crescent in the southeast. Communication and transportation were, moreover, quite primitive compared to today
– it took weeks for messages to travel from one province
to another distant province, and it could take even longer
for an army to reach trouble spots. More centrifugal than
this geographical span was the cultural and ethnic span; the

---

[29] <u>History of the Roman Empire</u> 7.6.1; in order to reflect Herodian's meaning, I
have translated his Greek somewhat loosely.

Roman Empire included numerous different peoples with numerous different cultures and languages.

While the Romans were consistently ruthless in crushing rebellion, they demonstrated considerable flexibility in how they incorporated and then administered conquered peoples. And they were remarkably tolerant of local cultures. Unlike the former Soviet Union, which attempted to justify and sweeten Russian domination of other peoples through compulsory indoctrination and comprehensive standardization, the Romans made their rule more palatable by tolerating a significant degree of diversity and even home rule. Over centuries their tendency was – and this is, of course, a simplification – to allow the older, more sophisticated cultures and peoples of the eastern Mediterranean to maintain their languages, cults, and ways of life and to run their own communities. This inclination was facilitated by the fact that Greek culture and the Greek language already dominated the eastern half of the Mediterranean because of early waves of Greek colonization[30] and because of Alexander the Great's more recent conquests.[31] Despite the occasional snotty swipe at Greeks, the Romans were comfortable with Greeks and Greek culture. Indeed, Roman high culture was almost completely derived from the Greek. Well-educated Romans were, in fact, bilingual; it was perfectly natural, for instance, that the second-century emperor Marcus Aurelius wrote his philosophical <u>Meditations</u> in Greek. This is not to say that the Romans had not affected the eastern half of the Empire culturally. The Roman army had a considerable presence in the east, and Roman gover-

---

[30] The western coast of Turkey, for example, had been dotted with Greek cities for centuries.

[31] The most prominent city of Roman Egypt, for example, was Alexandria, a foundation of Alexander's that was predominately Greek.

nors had the final say on all issues. The cult of Rome and the *genius*[32] of the Emperor was widespread and prominent. The most appealing features of Roman civilization, such as gladiatorial combat and aqueducts,[33] found a home in many communities in the east, as did many Roman businessmen and colonists.

The site of our story, Carthage, was in the western half of the Roman Empire, however. Things were different there, as the Romans confronted cultures (often Celtic or German) that they perceived to be more primitive, less civilized. Romanization followed. It is no accident that today most peoples of western continental Europe speak languages descended from Latin: French, Italian, Portuguese, and Spanish. The Romans certainly took action to "civilize" these primitive subjects, but the lion's share of this civilizing and romanizing seems to have taken place voluntarily. You do not really need to shove a bathhouse – complete with heated pools, steam bath, and massage – down the throat of an ancient Parisian shivering in January. The Romans also cleverly – and almost programmatically – co-opted local big shots throughout the Empire. The big shots acquired Roman citizenship, the prestige and influence of connections to their world's masters, and the comfort of knowing that those masters would preserve the wealth, privilege, and power they enjoyed in their hometowns. The Romans, in exchange, could feel confident that local moguls throughout the Mediterranean would see to order and loyalty, and, more often than not, enhance Rome's authority and grandeur through the promotion of Roman or romanized

---

[32] An untranslatable Latin word best rendered, perhaps, as "guardian spirit": it designates the emperor's spiritual/religious power and vitality that enable him to provide so much to his subjects.

[33] Modern city dwellers, too, love the accessibility of fresh water, and Russell Crowe and Ridley Scott have demonstrated the abiding attraction of gladiators.

cults, civic structures, institutions, and the like. Still, such manifestations of romanization tended to be more transformative in the western part of the Empire.

As the Greek language and culture dominated the eastern part of the Roman Empire, so the Latin language and Roman culture dominated the west. It was, of course, not so simple. The relative security of the Empire and the opportunities for travel and trade it provided, the ethnic complexity and often distant postings of the Roman army, and the vast ancient slave trade meant that peoples of the hundreds of ancient ethnicities represented in the Roman Empire wound up living and dying far from home. Nor did the dominant Roman and Greek cultures obliterate the innumerable native cultures of the Mediterranean. Some of these native peoples could even exploit the relative tranquility and unity of the Roman Empire to spread aspects of their culture. There was a lively marketplace, for example, of non-Roman religions and cults throughout the Empire, of which Christianity was only one competitor. The Egyptian cult of Isis traveled on the Empire's trade routes, the Iranian cult of Mithras along the marching routes of the army, and Christianity along both. The lines on the checkerboard were permeable, for ideas and customs as well as people.

Like most cities in the western part of the Roman Empire, Carthage was predominantly Latin in language and Roman in culture. Its history and its character in Perpetua's day were exceptional, however. Perpetua's Carthage was the distant descendent of <u>the</u> Carthage, home of both Dido, the tragic queen of Roman mythology driven to suicide when Rome's national hero Aeneas jilted her, and home of Hannibal, whose sensational crossing of the Alps and military genius threatened Rome's very existence until his defeat in 202 BCE. Colonists from Phoenician Tyre (part of modern-day Lebanon) founded the city around 800 BCE, and the outpost grew into one of the wealthiest and most powerful cities of the western Mediterranean. We use the term Punic to designate the Phoenician people and culture of Carthage, and their language.[34] Punic Carthage's powerful and wealthy were largely descended from those Semitic Phoenician colonists, but the pre-Punic African natives contributed significantly to the city's population and manpower; Carthage was ethnically mixed. Eventually Punic Carthage and Rome became rivals and struggled for dominance of the western Mediterranean. Despite her wealth, might, and leaders like Hannibal, Carthage was finally destroyed in 146 BCE.

It was not until about a century later that Julius Caesar refounded Carthage, but as a Roman colony with Roman settlers. Roman Carthage soon got considerable boosts when it became the capital of the province of Africa and when Caesar's grand-nephew and adoptive son Augustus sent veterans of his army to live there and promoted the rebuilding of the city. In defeating his Roman rivals for control of the Empire, Augustus had amassed an immense army, and peace meant that thousands and thousands of his veterans needed to be sent home, to their old ones, or to new ones like Carthage. Most of new Carthage was laid out according to Roman principles; indeed, the city was a jewel of Roman city planning. It grew and prospered. Even a disastrous fire in the second century was turned to advantage. Just as the Great Fire of 1666 provided King Charles II with the opportunity to recreate London, the burning of Carthage provided the emperors Antoninus

---

[34] The word "Punic" is derived from the Latin for Phoenician, *poenicus* or *punicus*. The Phoenicians of the western Mediterranean were the ones the Romans first and most significantly encountered.

Pius (r. 138-161 CE) and Marcus Aurelius (r. 161-180 CE) with the opportunity to rebuild the city's structures even more grandly. One should not imagine a ramshackle desert settlement like the Zucchabar of the movie "Gladiator."[35] By Perpetua's day, reconstructed and expanding Carthage had become one of the largest, wealthiest, most sophisticated, and splendid cities in the Empire – a Chicago or Los Angeles to Rome's New York – as the quotation from Herodian at the beginning of this section indicates.

And like those great cities of the United States, and like ancient Rome itself, Carthage was culturally and ethnically diverse. Augustus' original colony had not been planted in a desert, and the cosmopolitan city's vitality and prosperity attracted outsiders. Perpetua's Carthage had a thriving Jewish community, as a cemetery a few miles outside the city indicates. As one would expect in a rich port city of the Roman Empire, Greek was used in trade, and some Carthaginians probably used Greek as their first language; quite a few of the surviving magical tablets that were intended to curse enemies were written in Greek. This sophisticated city's liberally educated ruling classes would have studied Greek, and quite a few were completely at home with it. Carthage's greatest pagan writer, Apuleius, gave some of his speeches in Greek, doubtless to an audience that could understand. It is thus not surprising that in Saturus' dream, Perpetua speaks Greek. Literate Christians, too, would be expected to know some Greek, perhaps even enough to dream in the language.[36]

The most significant contribution to Carthage's cultural and ethnic population, however, came from the descendents

---

[35] Zucchabar actually existed; it was a Roman city in the African province of Mauretania.

[36] Some scholars have even argued that Perpetua's account was originally written in Greek and then translated into Latin. See "A Word on the Text" on page 99.

of the ancient Punic and pre-Punic Carthaginians.[37] The Romans had indeed destroyed the city in 146 BCE, but much of the Punic population remained in the area, as in the rest of north Africa, and they contributed to the evolution of Rome's African colonies, including Carthage. Roman Carthage was gifted with considerable territory populated with Punic towns, farms, and estates. As Carthage again became the center of the region, people from the surrounding area were drawn to it. The originally distinct Roman and Punic populations mixed, in every respect, and begat a racially mixed, cross-acculturated, composite urban citizenry that preserved significant elements and consciousness of Punic identity, despite deep romanization.[38] Some of the Latin-speaking Scillitan martyrs seem to have been products of this melding, to judge by their typically African names.[39]

Only Rome, perhaps, would have presented a more variegated, sophisticated, and important stage for the trial of Perpetua and her friends.

Persecution

> You have done exactly what you should have, my dear Pliny, in dealing with the cases of those who have been accused of being Christians before you. We simply can't establish a comprehensive policy that would determine a more or less fixed procedure. We should not go after them, but if they are accused and the case against them is made, they must be punished, but nonetheless under

---

[37] Through centuries of living together, intermarriage, and Punic dominance, the Phoenician and native elements of the area had blended, with Punic culture and language prevailing.

[38] Rives, <u>Roman Carthage</u> 100-172, gives an excellent analysis of this process in Carthage's religious life.

[39] See Rives, <u>Roman Africa</u> 114-121, for a discussion. The text of <u>The Acts of the Scillitan Martyrs</u> (including the names in question) is provided in Appendix 2.

this condition: if someone denies that he is Christian and proves that he is not by supplicating to our gods, his repentence should win him pardon, even if he had been suspected in the past. As you know, though, anonymous pamphlets should have no place in our legal system. For they provide the worst sort of precedent and do not belong in our age.

> – letter of the Emperor Trajan to his governor of Bithynia-Pontus, Pliny the Younger; <u>Letters</u> 10.99

Many these days are under the impression that the Romans constantly and brutally persecuted the early Christians; that tens of thousands, perhaps hundreds of thousands, of those Christians suffered ghastly deaths bearing witness to their faith; that some of those ancient believers managed to survive by hiding in catacombs from totalitarian Rome's dogged secret police. Some of this view may be attributed to old Hollywood movies that melodramatically and extravagantly depict the travails of Rome's Christians. And anyone reading late antique and medieval collections of saints' lives[40] readily could get the impression that martyrdom was the standard experience of early Christians. The thousands of often gory depictions of Christian martyrs in museums and churches (many of which are dedicated to martyrs) would seem to confirm that impression. It is, however, false.

In fact, persecutions were relatively infrequent, and when they did occur, tended to be of short duration and limited to few places. The first empire-wide persecution started in 249 CE, more than two centuries after Christianity's inception, approximately two centuries after the new religion had arrived in Rome itself, and almost a

---

[40] Jacopus de Voragine's immensely influential thirteenth-century <u>Golden Legend</u> is a prime example.

half century after Perpetua and her friends lost their lives. In Perpetua's own province of Africa, as far as we know, it was not until 180 CE that any Christians were executed for their faith.[41] Most Christians in most towns throughout the vast chronological and geographical span of the Roman Empire never had to choose between denying their faith and losing their lives.

The sporadic and localized nature of persecution suggests that the Roman government may have had no consistent or even clear policy on the Christians, and our sources bear this out. The famous correspondence between the Emperor Trajan and one of his provincial governors, Pliny the Younger, provides an illustration.[42]

Pliny recounted to the Emperor that he had dealt with several cases of provincials whose neighbors had denounced them as Christians:

> I asked them whether they were Christians. If they confessed, I asked them a second and third time, threatening them with the penalty. I ordered those who wouldn't budge to be executed. Nor did I have any doubt about this course, since their stubborness and inflexible obstinacy surely must be punished, regardless of the nature of what they confessed to.
>
> – Pliny, <u>Letters</u> 10.98

---

[41] Tertullian, in his <u>To Scapula</u> (<u>ad Scapulam</u>) 3.4. Scapula was governor of Africa about a decade after Perpetua's death. Writing about 40 years after Perpetua's death, the Christian writer Origen observed that only "few" Christians had died for their faith and that one could "easily count" them (<u>Against Celsus</u> [<u>contra Celsum</u>] 3.8).

[42] This is the same Pliny who was so pleased with his devoted wife. His letters are among our best sources of information about life among Rome's elite. Of particular interest is the extensive correspondence between him and the emperor Trajan; the exchange about the Christians belongs to this group. These letters were written when Pliny was governing the financially troubled province of Bithynia-Pontus in 111 CE, that is, almost a century before the martyrdom of Perpetua and her friends.

Some denouncers were encouraged by their success, and accusations proliferated; at some point an anonymous pamphlet with the names of suspected Christians appeared. The accused were brought before Pliny, and if they "repeated after me an appeal to the gods and...offered incense and wine to your image," he let them go, "if in addition they cursed Christ, none of which things, it is said, those who are really Christians can be forced to do." (Letters 10.98) Some accused did all this, but they also admitted that they had previously been Christians. Here Pliny ran into a problem. He did not really understand what the crime of being a Christian meant. Christians were suspected of committing ritual atrocities – including infanticide and cannibalism – and of staging incestuous orgies.[43] Were they subject to prosecution because it was assumed that Christians committed these heinous crimes? That would mean, in the eyes of the law, if you prove someone is a Christian, you have proven that she or he is a murdering fiend. And did the Christians actually do these ghastly things? Or was the issue that there was something intrinsically wrong about being a Christian, even if the Christian had led an otherwise law-abiding life? Pliny confessed to Trajan that he did not know the answers to these questions, and knowing was a matter of life and death for the accused.

In Pliny's view, the offering of incense and wine and the cursing of Christ proved that the accused either never had been or no longer was a Christian. If the crime was purely one of identity, that test solved the problem. But if Christians were liable to prosecution because of the unspeakable crimes their Christianity guaranteed that they had committed, should apostates be set free? No ancient

---

[43] More below on these accusations and their ramifications for the Christians (pp. 42-43).

serial-killer could say to a governor, "Yes, I was a very active murderer, but I stopped killing two years ago and am not into it anymore," and expect to go free. Surely no former Christian could be set free if he had slaughtered and eaten babies in a dark ritual, however strenuously he rejected that past and promised to dine more convention-ally in the future. And so Pliny investigated the cult. He found no atrocities and in his letter characterizes the new religion as harmless.[44] Not only had he realized that he did not understand the nature of the crime, but the number of the accused had grown quite large and threatened only to increase, and both women and children were also impli-cated, to Pliny's discomfort. For all these reasons, Pliny felt obliged to consult Trajan and got the response quoted at the beginning of this section.

Pliny's inquiry and Trajan's response have raised as many questions as they have answered about the legal status of the early Christians, as the voluminous, often conten-tious scholarship on the correspondence indicates. Let me state a few of these questions and offer answers that I hope will help clarify the Christians' situation.

• Neither Pliny nor Trajan mentions a specific law forbidding Christianity or any rationale for such a law, although we would certainly expect Trajan to refer to a law in answering Pliny's questions. Could it be that there was in fact no such law? For us, to be charged and punished for an activity that no specific statute forbids is an absurdity. Not

---

[44] Though he still labels it "a debased superstition carried to great lengths"; old mentalities die hard. The Latin term for superstition, *superstitio*, indicates either excessive religiosity (this would include superstition in our sense) or strange, foreign cult practices or doctrines. "The closest modern equivalent to this latter sense is 'cult' in the popular usage – a peculiar religion having its roots in mainstream religions but differing from them, or a religion imported from abroad." (Walsh, "Atheism" 260)

so for the Romans. We have the impression that Roman law was exceptionally detailed, comprehensive, and well reasoned – indeed, it is still studied in many law schools – but most of that law is civil, concerning lawsuits, property rights, inheritance, and the like. Roman criminal law, under which being a Christian would fall, was in fact relatively undeveloped. The authorities, especially in the provinces, had considerable leeway in governing Rome's subjects. In making decisions, they might cite laws, but then again they might not. Their primary responsibility was to maintain good order, and they did not require specific laws to take action, render judgments, or even exact punishments. This degree of provincial autonomy was perfectly natural and indeed necessary because the Roman Empire was huge and complex, and, as noted above, transportation and communication were terribly primitive and slow. If the emperors had not given their governors the freedom to render judgments independently, the empire could not have functioned. And so, to a significant extent, governors <u>were</u> the law in their own provinces; they did not need to find, cite, verify, or even understand laws in order to punish people.

• So was it essential that governors hear accusations against Christians and condemn them in order to preserve order? Pliny's letter and Trajan's response suggest that they did not view the Christians as dangerous. In urging the emperor to allow him to set Christian apostates free, Pliny argues,

> The infection of this supersition has spread beyond the cities all the way to the villages and the countryside, but I think it can be stopped and straightened out. It is pretty clear that the temples, which had been nearly deserted, have begun to be crowded again. Sacred rites that had been neglected for quite some time are experi-

encing a revival, while food for victims is selling again, although you couldn't find a buyer before this. All this makes it pretty obvious that a great many people can be reformed, if given the opportunity to repent. [45]

– <u>Letters</u> 10.98

This passage does suggest that Christianity is undesirable and that, at least in Pliny's province of Bithynia-Pontus, a checking of the new cult strengthens the old cults – surely a social good, in the view of the authorities, and one to be promoted. But Pliny's investigation had revealed that Christianity was essentially harmless and, more significant yet, Trajan explicitly ordered that the authorities "should not go after" the Christians. Assuredly, the Roman authorities would not have hesitated to root out brutally a movement they considered dangerous to or subversive of the social order. And, as indicated above, prosecutions and persecutions of the Christians were in fact few and far between.

The governors' considerable discretion could also work to the Christians' advantage. In the essay, <u>To Scapula</u>, Tertullian cites examples of governors who undermined attempts to prosecute Christians – one apparently contrived language whereby Christians could affirm their Christianity without suffering punishment – or who simply refused to hear their cases or to punish them (4, 5). Around 185 CE,

---

[45] The thronging of the temples has been adduced as evidence that butchers and other business folks invested in the apparatus of sacrifice were responsible for the accusations brought to Pliny (for the bibliography on the economic interests that might have been concerned about Christianity, see Walsh & Gottlieb, <u>Christen</u> 82, note 362). Possibly. But the accusors may have had a completely different agenda that brought about this happy – for certain merchants – result. In any event, it is difficult to see here any genuine or lasting pagan religious revival. It was surely insecurity and fear that impelled every provincial who was not a dedicated Christian to rush out to make a public statement of her or his non-Christianity.

Arrius Antoninus, governor of the province of Asia (essentially, the western coast of modern Turkey), was persecuting Christians. Tertullian tells us that when all the Christians in one town voluntarily offered themselves for martyrdom,[46] Arrius had a few executed but let the bulk of them go with the sly dismissal, "You miserable people, if you want to die, go find a cliff or a rope!" (5) By declining to punish those Christians, Arrius indicated that he considered Christianity more an irritation than a danger; nor did he feel compelled by law to punish them.[47]

• If there was no explicit law against Christianity on the books, and if the authorities did not consider the Christians dangerous, why would they, however occasionally, allow prosecutions and even executions? One answer is simply that their legal system permitted it. Romans and their provincial subjects could accuse anyone of pretty much anything. You could try to prosecute, say, shoemakers, just for being shoemakers, just as today anyone can file a lawsuit. However, your prospects for success would have been slim to none, and you might even earn yourself a beating for bringing something resembling what we would call a frivolous lawsuit. What made Christians different from shoemakers and other groups was the widespread sense (shared by the Roman authorities) that there was something wrong with them and, more critical yet, that there was precedent for prosecution and persecution. Roman governors regularly employed precedent in law and administration. Indeed, the application of precedent was indispensable to the running

---

[46] It is not entirely implausible that every single Christian came forward, but some exaggeration on Tertullian's part is suspected. It is also worth noting that the quotation is in Greek, although Tertullian wrote the <u>To Scapula</u> in Latin.
[47] And, in fact, the number of Christian martyrs before 249 CE seems to have been small; see above, note 41.

of the Roman Empire. Pliny's treatment of the Christians in Pontus, for example, offered a precedent to later governors who could find license to act against the Christians because Pliny had done so and Trajan had approved of his procedures. Christians, including Perpetua and her fellows, would again and again encounter variations on Pliny's sacrifice test. The fact that neither Pliny nor Trajan cited any law was irrelevant. None of our extant sources, unfortunately, explicitly and unambiguously cites a particular precedent as initiating persecution, any more than they cite any specific law or statute. We cannot, then, identify with certainty <u>the</u> precedent that first put Christians as Christians in jeopardy. The sources do, however, mention incidents that could have, individually or collectively, rendered being Christian essentially illegal. One such incident involved one of Rome's greatest disasters.[48]

In 64 CE, a catastrophic fire destroyed a huge swath of Rome. The city's desperate and frustrated inhabitants searched for a way to explain their misery, and for a scapegoat. Someone had to pay. Unfortunately for Nero, who was emperor at the time, suspicion fell on him. This was perfectly natural inasmuch as the emperors seemed to be arbiters of everyone's fate, guarantors of peace and prosper-

---

[48] Other candidates have been proposed. Fox, <u>Pagans</u> 430-432, discusses the possibility that St. Paul's trial in Rome, which he dates to around 61 CE (that is, before and unconnected to the persecution after the Great Fire in 64), set the precedent for the persecution of Christians. A. N. Sherwin-White's <u>Roman Society and Roman Law in the New Testament</u> (Oxford University Press, 1963) still provides a useful treatment of the legal issues behind Paul's arrest and imprisonment; Wansink, <u>Chained</u>, examines the incarcerations. Much remains uncertain, however, including precisely when and in what context he died. Another way to look at the issue is that a series of legal and extra-legal encounters between Christians, on the one side, and Roman or provincial authorities, on the other, cumulatively established precedent. The result was that Christians could be prosecuted for being Christians, but no authority could, or would need to, identify a single encounter or event as <u>the</u> precedent.

ity, and therefore responsible when things went wrong, too. A huge fire that cleared away Rome's slums would also have seemed a perfectly rational, though reprehensible, ticket to urban renewal, and who but the emperor could pull off such a massive razing and eviction?[49] Nero needed to deflect the blame onto someone else, and the Christians fit the bill. Christianity was a new, secretive, anti-social cult[50] suspected of ritual atrocities, some of whose members may have talked too enthusiastically about the world ending in conflagration while Rome was burning. Many Roman Christians, possibly including Peter and Paul, met their ends in sadistic public displays. This brutality ultimately revolted Rome's masses, even though our pagan source suggests that Rome's Christians were extremely unpopular:

> To stop the rumor (i.e. that he was responsible for the fire), Nero came up with scapegoats; he accused and sadistically punished those people the crowd calls "Christians," who were hated because of their reprehensible behavior. They were named after a certain Christus, who was executed by governor Pontius Pilate when Tiberius was emperor. Their pernicious superstition was temporarily suppressed, but it broke out again, not only in Judea, the evil's birthplace, but it reached Rome itself, a city packed with every disgusting and shameful thing that has poured into it from the whole world. First, then, the authorities would arrest those who confessed.[51] Then they used these people's testimony to convict a huge number, not really on the charge of arson, but because

---

[49] Nero built his "Golden Palace," a vast and spectacular villa set in artificially landscaped grounds, on urban land cleared by the fire. The Colosseum was later built on the location of the pond for this "country" estate. What remains of the Palace is under ground, but visitors can see a wing of impressive rooms with a guide in Rome today.

[50] In the modern usage; see above, note 44.

[51] Tacitus seems to mean that they confessed to being Christians, not to being arsonists.

of their hatred of humankind. And their deaths entailed ridicule: they were dressed in animal skins for dogs to savage, or they were crucified or set on fire; and at dusk they were burned to provide lamplight. Nero offered his own gardens for the spectacle, and this entertainment was presented in the circus too, where Nero, dressed like a charioteer, mixed with the crowd or stood in a chariot. Although the victims were guilty and deserved severe punishment, people started to pity them, since it was felt that they were being killed not for the public good but to satisfy the viciousness of one man alone.

– Tacitus, <u>Annals</u> 15.44

This persecution was limited to the city of Rome, and the Christians who died in it were actually executed as arsonists, but it established the mentality that the Christians were criminals and the precedent and policy that the authorities could take drastic action against them. The Christian cult's very origin, in Roman eyes, suggested that they should be subject to prosecution and execution: a Roman governor had crucified Christianity's founder in one of the empire's most turbulent provinces; it's no surprise that a criminal had founded a criminal organization. And so a provincial accusing someone of being a shoemaker would find himself confronted with a very irate governor,[52] but the accuser of Christians could well find an attentive and sympathetic ear.

• But doesn't Pliny's letter indicate that he actually punished the Christians because of "their stubbornness and inflexible obstinacy"? Yes, but this is a further indication of how much the Christians' fate depended on the attitudes and inclinations – at times, we suspect, the whims – of

---

[52] In actuality, of course, such an absurd allegation would never get to a governor; it is the principle behind the example that matters here.

Roman governors. At the time he wrote this letter, Pliny was uncertain about the particulars of the crime of being a Christian and about the appropriate punishment. He had come to feel uneasy about his own actions up to that point. He nonetheless states with complete confidence that their unwillingness to deny that they were Christians when he, the representative of Roman prestige and power, made it perfectly clear that they were to do so, merited punishment. By approving of Pliny's procedures, moreover, Trajan was saying, in effect, "Yes, regardless of what this is all about, we can't have people refusing to knuckle under to our authority."[53] The dozens of letters Pliny and Trajan exchanged reveal that both men were deeply concerned about the welfare of Rome's subjects and that they tried to rule humanely and justly. And in their exchange concerning the Christians, they were clearly searching for and, in their own view, found, a decent way of handling a complicated situation. At the same time, they did not hesitate to take severe, even drastic, action on grounds that twenty-first-century sensibilities would deem illegitimate and frivolous. Still, they took this action hesitantly and relatively infrequently.

• So, could Christians, except for some isolated incidents, rest easily in their beds? Unfortunately, no. Formal persecutions that resulted in torture and death were relatively infrequent. But no Christian living in peace could be certain that things would not change tomorrow; that some neighbor, incited by hatred of the cult, by self-interest, or perhaps even by the opportunity to indulge a personal grudge, might not set in motion a persecution; that a new governor, less sympathetic than his predecessor or even hostile to Christianity, might not welcome accusations against

---

[53] It is important to keep in mind that the Christians were not arrested because of their stubbornness; it became an issue only after their arrest.

Christians or, worse yet, even encourage them.[54] Many Christians, although in no immediate danger of losing their lives, were subject to unofficial (or, perhaps, informally sanctioned) harassment. Tertullian complains of soldiers blackmailing Christians, and "most of all, our meetings and gatherings are disrupted." (Apology 7.3-4) This occasional harassment in Carthage made day-to-day life more difficult and served as a reminder that at any moment more serious persecution was possible. Insecurity and apprehension were part of daily life. [55]

• Were other religious groups subject to the same strange (from our perspective) treatment and procedures? No. In the Roman Empire there was no other cult or religion quite like Christianity. There were a great many non-Roman cults that had spread throughout the Empire, but only Christianity and Judaism required their adherents to reject other gods and their worship. And, as we shall see below, pagan cults were entwined with so many other aspects of ancient life that rejection of those cults bordered on wholesale rejection of Greco-Roman society and culture. The Christians were also different from the Jews, who first and foremost were a <u>people</u>, and an ancient one at that; the Romans were inclined to allow for traditional national peculiarities, even ones like circumcision that they considered bizarre and distasteful. From the Roman point of view, the Christians were a <u>movement</u> without a traditional identity defined by ancestral customs. They merited no tolerance.

• Would all scholars of the persecutions agree with

---

[54] Perhaps one of the best examples of a governor encouraging persecution is Hilarianus, the governor who sentenced Perpetua and her friends to death; see note to section 6.3 in the text. For a comprehensive discussion see Rives, "Piety" 1-25.

[55] Christians in other communities were almost certainly victims of similar abuses.

this analysis? Absolutely not. There is little about early Christianity and its persecution that is not controversial. Check the "Recommended Reading" for books and articles that will give you fuller introduction to the debates and other interpretations of the sources.

Christianity, then, may have in effect been illegal without any specific law saying so, but the emperors, at least up to Perpetua's day, had shown little interest in doing anything about it. The issue was a local one. In the sporadic persecutions of Christians in the Roman Empire, the key players were provincials and their Roman governors, neither of whom were compelled or obliged by law, custom, or self-preservation to go after the Christians. Rather, their shared suspicions and resentments cast them in the roles of instigators of and abettors to persecution. To understand fully the causes of persecution, then, we must understand what it was about the Christians that induced some of their neighbors to take the brutal step of setting persecution in motion and/or enthusiastically supporting, even reveling in, cruel and humiliating executions.

Christian & Pagan in Carthage

> But look! Another crowd, just as numerous, elegant, and fashionable as those sitting, is coming out from the stands. Some bring baskets of bread, white napkins, and gourmet dishes; others serve wine cultivated to relax our limbs...ah, you would think them servants of the gods! You blessed man,[56] you nourish Rome's demanding, formally dressed elite, but you also feed so many so generously that no one need worry about the price of food. Come on, Good Old Days, compare this feast

---

[56] The poem addresses the emperor Domitian (r. 81-96), father of the feast.

to antiquity's Golden Age! Wine never flowed so lav-
ishly then, nor did harvest's fruits last so long. We all eat
together at one table: children, women, the rich, the poor,
and those between. We are all free of life's usual social
hierarchy. Even you join us, and every one, rich or poor,
whoever it is, can boast of sharing the banquet table with
the Emperor... Night was just approaching with its deep
blue when a blazing wheel ascended from the middle of
the sand to shine brightly through deep darkness... Its
flames lit up the sky, yielding not a whit to night's gloom.
Lazy Rest and sluggish Sleep take the hint and get out
of town. Who could possibly describe the spectacles, the
wild joking, the banquets, the free food, the vast rivers of
wine? I'm tiring out now... I've had a bit to drink, you
know... time to sleep...[57]

   – Statius, <u>Silvae</u>, I.6.28-50, excerpts, in praise of the
Roman winter solstice festival, the Saturnalia;
late 1st CE

Sounds like fun, doesn't it? There were few things,
if any, in the ancient world that provided as much joy as
pagan festivals did, especially for the great mass of human-
ity whose resources could procure only the most basic forms
of entertainment and pleasure. And the rhythm of Greco-
Roman life intensified the festivals' importance; since there
were no weekends, for most people the only holidays were
the festival holy days. In Perpetua's time, however, there was
a crimp in the party. The Christians, who had become a
significant and noticeable minority throughout the Roman
Empire and especially in cosmopolitan cities like Carthage,
would not participate – in fact, disapproved – and this sepa-
ration was a source of tension for pagans and Christians.
Let's look first at the pagan point of view.

---

[57] In translating this passage, I have changed some of the particulars of the Latin
in order to make the passage's sense clearer.

For all the delight ancient festivals provided, they were religious services intended to placate, thank, and maintain good relations with the gods. These relations were absolutely critical for society since, in the pagan view, the world was full of gods who determined success in war, agriculture, business, love – virtually every aspect of life; they could make or break individuals, communities, peoples. Would the gods resent the fact that a portion of the population refused to worship them? And would the entire community have to suffer the consequences? Many pagans might have been willing to overlook Christian separateness in normal times – theirs was no totalitarian society that monitored and compelled conformity of thought and behavior – but the Christians' absence from these festivals must have rankled in bad times, when plague, earthquake, war, or other catastrophes required a ratcheting up of sacrifice and supplication to address a desperate situation. It also rankled in the best of times, as when, just a few years before Perpetua's martyrdom, Carthage and other communities throughout the Roman Empire extravagantly celebrated the emperor Septimius Severus' resolution of a civil war and his restoration of peace. These outsiders in our midst, many must have thought, will neither share in helping the community during an emergency nor share our joy and relief when the state averts disaster and prospers.

Just as galling, I suspect, was the Christians' simple unwillingness to participate in cherished communal activities.[58] Irritation at others' refusal to go along with our favorite pastimes is by no means exclusively an ancient phenomenon. Those who drink sometimes resent those who don't; some students are irritated by colleagues who decline to go out and "party," seeing in the refusal an implied criticism. The desire

---

[58] For a discussion, with sources and bibliography, see Walsh & Gottlieb, <u>Christen</u> 25-27.

to impose conformity on others and the resentment of those who won't knuckle under is very much alive in our age.

Yet as much as we today may resent outsiders and kill-joys, the animosity was far more intense for ancient Romans. Many if not most twenty-first-century Americans have made home and family the center of their lives. This focus makes perfect sense in a society that cherishes a document that trumpets "life, liberty, and the pursuit of happiness," a trinity of essentially private, personal values and priorities. Our focus on the home makes even more sense considering how spacious, comfortable, and self-sufficient so many of our residences are; we don't even have to leave our homes to connect with the outside world – entertainment, information, commerce, and even romance are just a click away. It's easy for us to be indifferent to unsociable neighbors when we can lead busy and comfortable lives in our own homes with family, friends, and a welter of gadgets.

However, most Romans lived in cramped, dingy, dismal quarters that were too hot in summer and too cold in winter. The technological wonders of the Roman Empire, the remarkable aqueducts, stadiums, roads, and the like, contributed nothing to most apartments and houses, which were utterly devoid of conveniences and comfort, let alone household appliances. Even the impressive mansions of wealthy Romans stack up poorly against the standard middle class American home; your abode is very likely more comfortable than the palace of Septimius Severus.[59]

---

[59] The emperor Augustus worried about the temperature in his home because of his somewhat fragile health. For all his resources and power, he had to go to extreme, almost comical, lengths to stay warm in winter and cool in summer: "In winter, he would protect himself by wearing four tunics, a thick toga, an undershirt, a woolen vest, and heavy leg-wraps; in summer, he would sleep with his bedroom doors open and often out in the open by a fountain, and on top of this with someone fanning him." (Suetonius, <u>Augustus</u> 82)

It is quite understandable, then, that life in the Roman Empire, especially male life, was lived outdoors, in public, and in the company of others. Nor were people encouraged to seek fulfillment, meaning, and prosperity outside the context of their towns and cities. The greatest satisfaction and richness in life was to be found in the society of others, through participation in the life of the community. Intrinsic to that life, indeed, one could argue, the cornerstone of that life, were the Romans' innumerable religious observances, sacrifices, celebrations, and festivals. It is no surprise that the Christian refusal to participate was viewed as an insult, perhaps even an assault on the Roman way of life.

What were the Christians doing, anyway, hiding behind closed doors while every one else was celebrating together? In his defense of Christianity, Minucius Felix, very likely a fellow African and possibly even a contemporary of Perpetua, tells us the answer his pagan neighbors came up with:

> They [sc. the Christians] have recruited from the lowest dregs of society and women too, since they naturally tend to be credulous and flighty; from these sources they have assembled a mob of blasphemous conspirators, bound together by nocturnal meetings, ritual fasts, and unnatural dining, not for any religious rites, but rather for criminality. They are a shadowy and secretive people, silent in public but talkative in corners; they despise temples as though they were tombs, they spit on the gods, they ridicule our sacred rites...they mix together in a sort of religion of lust, and they indiscriminately call each other brother and sister, so that they can exploit these honored names to convert normal sex into incest... Reports of their initiation ceremony are as disgusting as they are notorious. They cake an infant in flour in order to deceive the unsuspecting; then they put the child before the initiate, who is told to strike the flour with

apparently harmless blows. The initiate thus unknow-
ingly kills the infant with wounds that are concealed.
I shudder to reveal this – but they thirstily lap up the
blood; they rip the child's body apart with zeal. They
make a covenant over this victim, and their complicity
in the atrocity binds them to mutual silence...

– <u>Octavius</u>, excerpts from sections 8-9

Incest, murder, even cannibalism – in the view of some
pagans, it was lurid and ghastly criminality that compelled
Christians to "shun the light" and keep their mouths shut in
public. Indeed, the only public expressions of this depravity
seemed to be the ridicule of decent pagan worship.[60]

Not all pagans who disapproved of or even hated
their Christian neighbors believed the rumors of ritual
atrocities, but there were plenty of other reasons to dislike
them, in addition to their self-imposed separateness. Some
considered Christians bad for business – just think of all
the folks who had an economic interest in pagan festivals:
priests, makers and peddlers of souvenir and devotional
statues, performers, farmers (all that sacrificing and feast-
ing!), manufacturers of the paraphernalia of sacrifice and
the materials of the shows, just to mention a few. And how
many pagans would the Christians' aggressive anti-pagan
invective provoke? In his <u>Apology</u>, most probably composed
only a few years before Perpetua's martyrdom, Tertullian
described a pagan celebration in terms very different from
those Statius used to characterize the Saturnalia:

---

[60] The classic examination of the charges of Christian ritual atrocities is F. J.
Dölger's "Sacramentum infanticidii," <u>Antike und Christentum</u> 4 (1934) 188-
228. See, too, A. McGowan, "Eating People: Accusations of Cannibalism
against the Christians in the Second Century," <u>Journal of Early Christian Studies</u>
2 (1994) 413-442, and James Rives, "Human Sacrifice among Pagans and
Christians," <u>Journal of Roman Studies</u> 85 (1995) 65-85.

So this is why Christians are public enemies, because they will not give the emperors meaningless, fake, thoughtless honors; because as people of true religion they celebrate the emperors' festivals in the heart rather than in revels. A fine sort of service that is, to bring braziers and dining couches into the streets to have a feast! To make the city look like a bar! To spill so much wine that the streets turn to mud! To run around in packs after violence and aggression and sex! How can such behavior be appropriate for the emperors' festive days, when we frown on it for other days? And it is we Christians who deserve to be condemned!? Why do we perform our vows and celebrate our joy in the Caesars with chastity, sobriety, and decency? Why on the day of celebration don't we hang laurel on our doors and impose daylight with our lamps? When a great public event calls, is it a respectable person's obligation to decorate the home like a whorehouse? We Christians are accused of an additional sacrilege because we will not join you in celebrating the holidays of the Caesars in an immodest, indecent, and promiscuous manner!

– 35.1-5, excerpts

Tertullian goes beyond defending and explaining his own position, the conventional agenda of an ancient Apology, and attacks paganism and pagans with considerable relish.[61] And perhaps to ill effect. Think how people today might bridle if their cheerful but gaudy Christmas

---

[61] Apologies in the ancient world were explanations or justifications of one's view or self. They were generally not very apologetic, in our terms, but tended to be aggressive. The most famous ancient example, indeed a model for all Apologies ancient and modern, was Plato's version of Socrates' defense of his life. Plato's Socrates speaks without a hint of regret, and the offensiveness of his defense induced some jurors who had voted to acquit him to vote for the death penalty. Socrates was also the model pagan martyr; it is not surprising that Perpetua's posture after her arrest resembles Socrates' in several respects, and she even plays the role of Socratic interrogator, as we shall see, when her distraught father begs her to save her life (3.1-2).

decorations were described as making their homes resemble whorehouses!

The passage just cited from Tertullian gives us a sense of how some Christians of Perpetua's day viewed pagan festivals, but we get only an inkling of how profoundly and divisively the festivals, and other aspects of the pagan world too, challenged early Christians. Whatever Christians anticipated in the next life, they first had to live in this world, a world that often seemed to be conspiring to make living a faithful and upstanding life impossible. Indeed, most forms of public entertainment – chariot racing, theater, professional athletics – existed as crucial elements of pagan religious festivals; whether Marius the Roman guy in the street was conscious of this or not, when he would wildly yell encouragement to his favorite charioteer or cringe at the crashes, he was participating in a religious service, going to church, we might say. Christians could not, of course, worship pagan deities, and this fact made the festivals extremely problematic. But how drab was life without them? We should keep in mind that there was no internet, no television, no movies, no iPods, no magazines (most people couldn't read anyway) to divert Romans, and the rest of life was replete with unpleasantness – no window screens, plenty of mosquitoes; clueless doctors, plenty of disease; no refrigerators, plenty of bad food (in both senses). And no weekends. Need Christians trudge though life without enjoyment? And, anyway, what is the harm in enjoying entertainment that is not intrinsically pagan, despite its context? It makes sense to categorize animal sacrifice as a purely and exclusively pagan activity;[62] employing elaborate rituals to slaughter animals is not part of normal,

---

[62] By Perpetua's day, the Temple in Jerusalem had been destroyed, and animal sacrifice had ceased to be an element of Jewish worship.

non-religious life. But racing – foot, horse, or chariot – is a human activity with no inherent religious content; children, after all, race spontaneously, almost unconsciously. As long as Christians preserve their fear of God, surely he does not object to their having some fun, especially since the instruments and materials of this fun are part of God's own good creation. Besides, though God has explicitly told humankind plenty of things to avoid, such as murder, adultery, and fraud, nowhere in Scripture can you find: "Thou shalt not go to the horse races, nor to the theater; thou shalt not view athletic competitions, nor contests."[63] Surely Christians could be faithful and still enjoy the communal activities the non-Christian environment provides.

The seductiveness of these and other arguments, often presented by his fellow Christians, compelled Tertullian to dedicate an entire essay, <u>On Shows</u>, to refuting them. Clearly some, perhaps many, Christians <u>were</u> attending the shows and availing themselves of other pleasures with pagan associations. Some thought this was just fine and said so. Or perhaps they found themselves unable to resist the temptations that beckoned, and so they manufactured justifications to assuage their consciences and silence curmudgeons like Tertullian. Nor did temptations end with the close of a festival.

Every day, the Christians' entire environment seemed to them aimed at tempting them to sin. Romans winked at marital infidelity (in men, at any rate), and sex with prostitutes was acceptable as long as not engaged in excessively. Masters had whatever kind of sex they wished with whatever kind of slaves they owned. All this was at odds

---

[63] This is a translation of an actual pseudo-commandment that Tertullian made up to illustrate the sorts of arguments adduced by Christians who wanted to attend the festivals (<u>On Shows</u> [<u>de spectaculis</u>] 3). The word translated here as "contest" is *munus*; it is at a *munus* that Perpetua and her fellow martyrs lost their lives.

with Christian teaching, and yet it was alluring. How can one live at odds with the dominant, ubiquitous culture, especially when that culture's enticements insidiously undermine your resolve and daily threaten to make you complicit in its laxity? The dilemma is very much alive today. Modern Christians who hope to abide by the prescriptions of the Bible and the convictions of their churches can find it difficult to withstand the pressures and temptations of a wider culture thoroughly at odds with their faith. Should they avoid the ubiquitous respectable hotel chains that provide and profit from pay-per-view pornography? Should they send their children to schools where plagiarism and sexual activity are the norm, and where students who do not conform may suffer ridicule and worse? Christians, of course, are not the only ones who find the way of the world in troubling conflict with their preferred way of life and values. Should anti-pornography feminists also avoid the pornography-peddling hotels? As with paganism in the Roman Empire, consumerism pervades our own public spaces, informs our consciousness and values, and provides our most prized pleasures. It is really not so surprising that one of President Bush's responses to the attacks of 9/11 was to urge us to go shopping. Many of us embrace commercial culture; others find it simultaneously alluring and repellent; still others are just appalled by it. It is nonetheless impossible to avoid, regardless of where we stand. How does one live in it without becoming of it?

One answer is to leave it. For Perpetua and other Christians of the Roman Empire, martyrdom was the most extreme expression of alienation from the world around them, the most extreme reaction to the problem of living in a culture hostile to, dangerous to, and subversive of their chosen life and convictions. They should not seek martyrdom, as we shall see, but they could embrace it, should it come their way.

Martyrdom

> Farewell, vain world! I'm going home!
> My savior smiles and bids me come,
> And I don't care to stay here long!
> Sweet angels beckon me away,
> To sing God's praise in endless day,
> And I don't care to stay here long!
> – American Traditional[64]

Some accounts of Christian martyrs suggest that for them martyrdom under the Roman authorities was, essentially, a no-brainer. If you were a believer, if you were part of this new community and had adopted this new way of life, it was simply a given that you would sacrifice your life when the call came and that you would do so utterly without hesitation and even with a good deal of cheer. At times martyrs seem not to have given their situation even a second thought. These depictions of early Christian martyrs eagerly embracing their fate can make them seem extraordinarily brave. Or not brave at all. Their apparent lack of doubt and reluctance, their unwavering and enthusiastic determination can almost lead the reader to suspect that the martyrs had never actually made a decision to give their lives, that their willingness to die was automatic, unthinking, almost devoid of the trepidation that makes heroes human and so compelling.

The reality, as so often is the case, was more complex.

---

[64] One can hear the hymn – and hearing intensifies its sentiment – on the soundtrack from the movie, <u>Cold Mountain</u>, or in the movie itself.

Like Christians today, Christians in 203 CE dedicated a good deal of energy to arguing with and reprimanding each other. Over 140 years earlier, Paul had written to the Christian community at Corinth in hopes of quelling their heated quarrels, and such disagreements and disputes continued to be an aspect of Christian life in Perpetua's day as well. Controversies could arise pertaining to internal matters, such as who has authority in a congregation, but many of the most vexing issues arose because Christians were living in a world at odds with their values and, periodically, at war with their faith. One of these controversies concerned how to respond to persecution, and not all Christians were on the same page.

There were (and are) several possible responses:

• A Christian could go forth and meet persecution. We have encountered an example of such "voluntary martyrdom" [65] above in the entire Christian community that presented itself to the governor Arrius Antoninus for execution. While courageous, this response posed a mortal danger to the soul; it came dangerously close to suicide, perfectly acceptable to pagan Romans but forbidden to Christians, whether Roman or not. Voluntary martyrs may also have endangered their fellow Christians by bringing attention to the Church at times when any sensible Christian would want to keep a low profile. The aggressive and perhaps even ostentatious manner of some voluntary martyrs very likely irritated pagans, particularly the authorities. The emperor Marcus Aurelius deplored the "melodrama" of Christian martyrs,[66] doubtless downright histrionic in the case of

---

[65] The term G. E. M. de Ste. Croix employed to characterize this phenomenon has become virtually a technical term ("Why Were the Early Christians Persecuted?" <u>Past and Present</u> 26 [1963] 21-24).

[66] <u>Meditations</u> 11.3.

voluntary martyrs, and these exhibitions would not have helped quench the anti-Christian passions that fueled the persecutions. And so, some church authorities and writers condemned voluntary martyrdom. Even the author of the Martyrdom of Saint Polycarp, although overflowing with admiration for martyrs and martyrdom, condemns voluntary martyrdom: "That is why, my brothers, we do not approve of those who volunteer themselves, since this is not what the Gospel teaches."(4) [67]

• A Christian could forbear, if persecution came her way. This path enabled the Christian to avoid exacerbating the persecution and falling into the grave sin of suicide, while standing by and up for the faith. The Christian should not thrust herself in front of the authorities, but if arrested, should not compromise either. Perpetua and most of her friends took this option.

• If persecution seemed imminent, the Christian could flee. When the persecution ended, as they all inevitably did, she could return home. This response had the advantage of allowing Christians to increase greatly their chances of survival without denying their faith. Those who escaped could even adduce the Gospel of Matthew as scriptural warrant: "When they persecute you in one town, flee to the next; for truly, I say to you, you will not have gone through all the towns of Israel, before the Son of man comes."(10.23) Many did flee, including priests and bishops, and even the great martyr Polycarp, mentioned above:

> Now at first when the most admirable Polycarp heard of this [i.e. persecution], he was not disturbed and even decided to stay in Smyrna; but most people advised

---

[67] The Martyrdom of Polycarp is universally regarded as authentic. Polycarp met his end in Smynra (modern Izmir in Turkey) around 155 CE (although the date is debated), about 50 years before Perpetua and her friends met theirs.

him to slip out quietly. And so he left secretly for a small estate on the outskirts, staying there with a few friends.(5)

Unsurprisingly, other Christians derided flight as weakness, if not cowardice, and more seriously as an indication of lack of faith in God. These critics quoted Jesus' Sermon on the Mount: "Blessed are you when men revile you and persecute you and utter all kinds of evil against you falsely on my account. Rejoice and be glad, for your reward is great in heaven, for so men persecuted the prophets who were before you." (5.11-12) Our friend Tertullian even wrote an essay, "On Flight in Times of Persecution," in which he argued that God wills all, including persecution, and so it is to be embraced, not avoided, as it tests and strengthens the faithful. He is accordingly very hard on those who flee, particularly priests and bishops, calling them wicked shepherds (11), and even opines that the agonies of one martyr, Rutilius, who had fled before ultimately being arrested, were a punishment for his earlier flight!(5)[68]

• A fourth response was to avoid arrest by bribery or some other chicanery. Roman and provincial officials, as well as the soldiers who carried out their orders, were notorious for their greasy palms. Through bribery, a Christian could save her life without having to deny her faith. In later persecutions, such practices were widespread. In the first empire-wide persecution starting in 249 CE under the emperor Decius, the authorities issued certificates that verified that people had sacrificed to the gods (and thus

---

[68] In an earlier work, To My Wife (ad uxorem), Tertullian allowed for flight (though with a noticeable lack of enthusiasm): "Why, even in persecution it is better to take advantage of this allowance, and to 'flee from town to town,' rather than, arrested and tortured, to deny the faith."(1.3) On Flight in Times of Persecution (de fuga in persecutione) belongs to Tertullian's Montanist phase.

had never been or no longer were Christians). Christians illicitly purchased these certificates in large numbers to save their lives without having to imperil their souls. Or so they hoped. As one would expect, many other Christians considered this path dishonorable, even sinful, and it could have consequences for the entire faith, undermining Christian claims of superior rectitude and thus dealing a blow to Christianity's credibility among pagans. Some Christians employed bribery to save their lives and souls in Perpetua's day as well, and Tertullian even mentions entire congregations buying off persecutors.[69] Disgusted, he compared this practice to "buying Christ."

• A Christian arrested and confronted with the potentially fatal question, "Are you a Christian?" could simply answer "No" and sacrifice to the gods as ordered. This Christian could then go free and continue to live as a Christian, but life was not so easy for these temporary apostates. They would have to admit they had grievously sinned, ask for forgiveness, and endure a public penance that most likely was very difficult and humiliating. Or they could argue that it was perfectly acceptable to deny the faith under extreme circumstances, that their public but insincere apostasy was no sin at all. The second-century Gnostic Christian writer Basilides of Alexandria was said to have advocated "carefreely denying the faith in times of persecution."[70] Heracleon, another second-century Gnostic Christian, distinguished confession by faith and conduct from verbal confession, that is, what is in your heart and how you live vs. the confession at trial – and to Heracleon, it is the former that counts. He even seems to argue that if a person's life and belief reflect his Christianity, then it is impossible for him

---

[69] <u>On Flight in Times of Persecution</u> 1.3.

to deny the faith, no matter what he says under duress.[71]
This application of Euripides' famously infamous line, "My
tongue took the oath, but my heart didn't,"[72] may seem
frivolous, a lame adult version of crossing your fingers when
making a commitment. From the safety of our twenty-first-
century armchairs, it is easy to dismiss these and other such
arguments for denying the faith as clever appeals to human
frailty, justifications that enabled Christians to do what they
so desperately wanted to do, although they were aware it was
wrong. However, ancient Christian advocates of martyrdom
took the arguments seriously and considered them a threat
to the backbone of the faith.[73] And no wonder. The stakes
were exceedingly high: life and death (in this world and the
next), the content of a Christian's character,[74] the vitality of

---

[70] Eusebius, The History of the Church 4.7. Gnosticism is an umbrella term
covering a wide variety of Christian sects that an emerging orthodoxy came
to consider heretical; indeed, some of the Gnostics' opponents asserted that
they were not Christians at all, and some Gnostics did seem to have at most
a tenuous connection to Christianity. Common to many Gnostic sects was a
reliance on knowledge revealed only to adherents. This knowledge was the key
to salvation (and everything else). Gnostics tended to despise the material world,
including their bodies, a tendency that apparently led to asceticism in some and
libertinism in others. It is difficult, though, to assess the accuracy of our sources
on Gnosticism, since they are mostly Christian polemicists. The bibliography
on Gnosticism is immense; a good place to start is Pheme Perkins' article in
The Encyclopedia of Early Christianity 2nd edition, vol. 1, ed. Everett Ferguson
(Garland, 1997) 465-470.
   Basilides of Alexandria taught in the second century and wrote a Gospel
(an analysis, not a narrative) and Psalms, but only fragments survive (for which,
see W. Foerster, Gnosis: A Selection of Gnostic Texts, vol. 1 [Oxford University
Press, 1972] 59-83).
[71] Fragment 50 (page 102) in A. E. Brooke, The Fragments of Heracleon (Texts
and Studies 1.4, 1891); Brooke has assembled the little that survives of Hercleon's
writings, although he does not provide an English translation.
[72] Hippolytus, line 612.
[73] Around the time of Perpetua's martyrdom, Tertullian provides an example. He
dedicated a work to refuting these arguments and to attacking their proponents.
Its title, Scorpiace, reveals how pernicious he considered them to be; they were, in
his view, poisonous scorpions.
[74] See Martin Luther King's great "I Have a Dream" speech (delivered 28 August
1963).

the Church. And Christian struggles with how to respond to persecution provoked and still provoke the troubling question of why a God of mercy and love could want, much less allow, his children to endure horrible suffering on his behalf. In his historical novel <u>Silence</u>, a meditation on the seventeenth-century Japanese authorities' attempt to eliminate Japan's then burgeoning Christian community, Shusaku Endo tells how the authorities would try to get Christians to trample on a bronze image of Christ, the <u>fumie</u>, and so publicly renounce their faith, a scenario remarkably similar to Roman authorities trying to get Christians to curse Christ and sacrifice to the gods.[75] Endo's protagonist is a priest who hears the groans of other Christians being tortured, and he has been informed that his apostasy will put an end to that torture. The priest's dilemma is even more vexed than Perpetua's, for his constancy was causing others to suffer as well. Endo narrates his moment of betrayal:

> "It is only a formality. What do formalities matter?" The interpreter urges him on excitedly. "Only go through with the exterior form of trampling." The priest raises his foot. In it he feels dull, heavy pain. This is no mere formality. He will now trample on what he has considered the most beautiful thing in his life, on what he has believed most pure, on what is filled with the ideals and the dreams of man. How his feet ache! And then the Christ in the bronze speaks to the priest: "Trample! Trample! I more than anyone know of the pain in your feet. Trample!
>
> It was to be trampled on by men that I was born into this world. It was to share men's pain that I car-

---

[75] There are other suggestive similarities as well. Particularly noteworthy is the application of torture coupled with apparent concern for the welfare of the persecuted (as the authorities saw it). In both cases the authorities were usually not intent on killing or brutalizing Christians, but on compelling public denial; and so strategies of persuasion, all too often violent, were devised to effect this.

ried my cross." The priest placed his foot on the <u>fumie</u>. Dawn broke. And far in the distance the cockcrew.[76]

Has Endo's priest convinced himself that Jesus would want him to end the suffering of others that his resistance is causing? Has he actually come to a deeper, truer understanding of Jesus' love for humankind? Or has the Jesus of mercy actually spoken to him? And yet, "the cock crew."[77]

• Or, finally, a Christian hauled before the authorities could genuinely deny and abandon the faith, never to return. Our Christian sources indicate that a great many did just that.

Perpetua and her fellow martyrs had other options, then, options that many Christians in their position exercised, options for which they could find plausible justification in Christian texts, options that might have saved their lives. Perpetua and her friends were no more automatons than was Jesus in the Garden of Gethsemane:

> Then Jesus went with them to a place called Gethsemane; and he said to his disciples, "Sit here, while I go yonder and pray." And taking with him Peter and the two sons of Zebedee, he began to be sorrowful and troubled. Then he said to them, "My soul is very sorrowful, even to death; remain here, and watch with me." And going a little farther he fell on his face and prayed, "My Father, if it be possible, let this cup pass from me; nevertheless, not as I will, but as thou wilt." (Mt 26:36-39)

---

[76] Shusaku Endo, <u>Silence</u> (trans. William Johnson; Taplinger Publishing Company, 1969/1980) 171.

[77] For an enlightening meditation on Endo's novel, see Stephen Fowl, "Paul's Reposte to Fr. Rodrigues: Conceptions of Martyrdom in Philippians and Endo's <u>Silence</u>," in <u>Postmodern Interpretations of the Bible</u> (ed. A. K. M. Adam; Chalice Press, 2001) 243-53.

Like Jesus, Perpetua and her companions made a choice. And again like Jesus, they were not without apprehension and fear, as the <u>Passion</u> indicates, despite their confidence and conviction.

The cost of avoiding martyrdom was, in the view of many Christians, extremely high, in this life as well as the next. The positive benefits of enduring martyrdom were correspondingly high.

To encourage their fellow Christians to endure martyrdom, some Christian writers trumpeted its rewards. <u>Whether</u> we will die is not the issue – contrary to what the apostate's cowardice and temporizing seem to suggest, we all die eventually – but <u>how</u> we die and the consequences of the manner of our death. The martyr's death earns her a second baptism, a cleansing of sins, and salvation, and Paradise. Christians were encouraged, moreover, to view the embrace of martyrdom as an imitation of Christ,[78] which should be every Christian's goal, and even as participation in his suffering. And it was a great victory; it is no surprise that athletic and military imagery occurs again and again in <u>Passions</u> and in essays and sermons regarding it. For triumph in those fields of endeavor entails considerable sacrifice, endurance, pain, and even – commonly in the case of the solider – death.[79] Most ancients considered victory in war and athletics well worth the cost. To Christians, the meaning and

---

[78] Jesus' example helped Christians find a middle course in terms of responding to persecution. In that he accepted his selfless death passively and quietly, he discouraged voluntary and melodramatic martyrdom; in that he chose death and defied the authorities when questioned, he encouraged his followers to endure suffering and death without equivocation or compromise.

[79] Ancient athletics not infrequently resulted in death as well. Greco-Roman contact sports (boxing, wrestling, and a combination of both plus a bit of judo called pankration) were brutal. In one of her visions, Perpetua winds up fighting with an Egyptian in the pankration (section 10: see the note to that passage for explanation of the sport).

glory of the martyr's victory were infinitely greater than those of war heroes and Olympic victors, even in this world. Their Christian contemporaries accorded them admiration, wonder, and veneration, and even began to attribute miraculous powers to them and to their bodies.[80] Recollection of their deeds became part of the religious life of subsequent Christian generations, as the survival and popularity of Perpetua's Passion indicates, and their names were immortalized on calendars, like those of ancient Olympic victors. Too, as we have seen, advocates of martyrdom could adduce scriptural passages, the ultimate authority, to shore up their case. The Gospel of Matthew proclaims, "Blessed are you when men revile you and persecute you and utter all kinds of evil against you falsely on my account" and "He who finds his life will lose it, and he who loses his life for my sake will find it."(Mt. 5.11 & 10.39) You will find elements or reflections of most of these inducements, in one form or another, in Perpetua's Passion.

And yet, despite the benefits that many Christians saw in suffering martyrdom, and despite the fears they had concerning the costs of denying their faith, many Christians failed when put to the test. Why did Perpetua, Saturus, and their friends, motley in their gender, class, education, and position in the Christian community, persist in their conviction unto death, when so many others faltered? What was it about them, and about others of remarkable courage, that enabled them to face unbearable suffering and death rather than renounce their faith? The Passion itself may provide some answers.

---

[80] See Fox, Pagans 446-450.

Perpetua

by Ann LoLordo

The ladder held all manner of things,
spears and hooks and knives,
but I was not deterred,
not by the serpent's tooth or its venom,
for I knew beyond lay my welcome.

A garden with all manner of fruit
and flora, passion fruit and pomegranates,
prickly pears and plums, the dark red center
of my heart. My father had hoped I would renounce
my faith and be freed from the prison
at Carthage, to leave the arena unscathed,
for the sake of my son. But this is the beginning
of my flowering, to rise up and embrace
language, which will free me
from earth's fever and its dark red scent.
Even now, as they oil my body, I am anxious
to be done with all manner of the body,
for though it is comely, it is no longer mine
to give. Felicity and I go together
to take up the bough of golden apples

and leave our children, a son and a daughter,
to retell the story I write today, in my own words.

Felicity, pin up your hair, gather your robe,
kiss me well, the Gate of Life is opening.

This poem is part of a collection of poems – focused on Perpetua and Felicity – by Baltimore-based poets. The collection in its entirety may be found in Appendix IV.

Perpetua's Passion: The Translation

■

1. If ancient examples of faith that testify to God's grace and serve the edification of humankind have been written down so that in reading and visualizing them we might honor God and strengthen ourselves, why shouldn't new examples, equally applicable to these two goals, also be set down?[1] (2) Surely the more recent things too will eventually

---

[1] This section by the editor of Perpetua's Passion reflects the controversies in Perpetua's day about the validity of contemporary (to them) prophecy and visions, and about how Christians should respond to persecution. Some Christians claimed that their visions and prophecies (and other ecstatic experiences like speaking in tongues) were inspired by the Holy Spirit and thus merited the acknowledgment of other Christians. In Phrygia (in modern day Turkey), starting around 165-170 CE, a man named Montanus and two women, Priscilla and Maximilla, made this claim, and their followers came to be known as Montanists. In his introduction to the Passion, the editor makes what can be seen as a programmatic Montanist statement, arguing that Perpetua's visions and martyrdom reflect the genuine working of the Holy Spirit and thus deserve the authority and respect accorded to scriptural descriptions of these phenomena. Indeed, the editor seems to imply that since her visions are nearer to the end times than those found in the New Testament, they have even greater authority. Other Christians viewed with suspicion contemporary claims of direct divine inspiration of these sorts, and their rejection of the New Prophecy, as it was called, ultimately prevailed. (For more on the Montanists, and particularly its response to persecution, see the Introduction, p. 15, note 22. Useful, too, are Jaroslav Pelikan, "Montanism and Its Trinitarian Significance" Church History 25.2 (June, 1956) 99-109, and Klawiter, "Priestly Authority" 251-261.

become ancient and essential to future generations, even though in their own present time they are accorded little authority because of the presumed veneration of antiquity. (3) But those who think that the one power[2] of the one Holy Spirit is bound to historical periods should realize that later events, being the most recent, ought to be considered even greater, in accordance with the abundance of grace decreed for the end times. (4) For, "In the last days, says the Lord, I will pour out my Spirit upon all flesh, and their sons and daughters will prophesy, and on my menservants and my maidservants I will pour out my Spirit, and the young men will see visions, and the old men will dream dreams."[3] (5) And so, just as we recognize and honor prophecies, we also recognize and honor the promised recent visions, and we regard the other workings of the Holy Spirit as support for the Church; for it is to the Church that the Holy Spirit was sent to hand out gifts to everyone, insofar as the Lord distributes to each and every one. And so we must write these things down and, through reading, celebrate them for the glory of God. This will keep the weak or despairing of faith from believing that divine grace was present only among the ancients, in the esteem either for martyrs or for visions. For the fact is that God always carries out his promises, as proof for non-believers and as aid to believers.

---

[2] *Virtutem* (accusative case; *virtus* in the nominative), which has several meanings, including courage, bravery, vigor, and excellence. The context and early Christian usage suggest that above all "power" and "efficacy" best render the *virtus* of the Holy Spirit in this passage. It can also mean "miracles," that is, manifestations of power. (Chirat, <u>Dictionnaire</u> 851, lists the possibilities and provides examples.)

[3] A translation of Acts 2:17-18. The setting for the passage in Acts is the Pentecost; Peter is speaking, and he cites the words of the prophet Joel: "And it shall come to pass afterward, that I will pour out my spirit on all flesh; your sons and your daughters shall prophesy, your old men shall dream dreams, and your young men shall see visions. Even upon the menservants and maidservants in those days, I will pour out my spirit." (Joel 2:28-29)

(6) Brothers and children, "what we have heard and touched with our hands we proclaim also to you, so that you" who were involved can recall the glory of the Lord and so that those who are now learning of it through word of mouth "may have fellowship with"[4] the holy martyrs, and through them with our Lord Jesus Christ, whose glory and honor are forever and ever. Amen.

2. Some young catechumens[5] were arrested: Revocatus and his fellow slave Felicity, and Saturninus and Secundulus. Among those arrested was Vibia Perpetua, a woman of a highly respectable family, who was also liberally educated and properly married. (2) Her father and mother were alive, as were two of her brothers, one of whom was a catechumen just like her. She also had an infant son, still at the breast, (3) and was herself around twenty-two years of age.[6] From this

---

[4] A distillation of 1 John 1:1-3: "That which was from the beginning, which we have heard, which we have seen with our eyes, which we have looked upon and touched with our hands, concerning the word of life – the life was made manifest, and we saw it, and testify to it, and proclaim to you the eternal life which was with the Father and was made manifest to us – that which we have seen and heard we proclaim also to you, so that you may have fellowship with us; and our fellowship is with the Father and with his Son Jesus Christ."

[5] Catechumens were those preparing and studying for full membership and participation in the Christian community. This stage could last as long as three years.

[6] Beyond these statements, we do not have much information on Perpetua's background and life before arrest, and so historians have had to draw inferences from the Passion to fill out her biography. She was certainly a member of a local elite, and Barnes, Tertullian 70, even suggests that her family may have been senatorial, that is, part of the Empire's loftiest class. The Greek translation of the Passion asserts that the martyrs were arrested in Thuburbo Minus, a significant Roman town about thirty miles west of Carthage that Augustus had founded for his veterans over two hundred years before Perpetua's death. Like Carthage, Thuburbo started as a Roman outpost in a sea of Punic and African settlement and so had been washed by those waters. Some of those who are convinced that the Latin text is the original version and that the Greek is a translation of it (for bibliography arguing the reverse, see "A Word on the Text," pp. 99) may view the statement about Thuburbo Minus as a later

point on, the entire narrative of her martyrdom was written by her in her own hand and reflects her own feelings.[7]

Perpetua's account of her ordeal follows.

3. While we were under guard, my father wanted to dissuade me and out of love kept trying to break my resolution.[8] I said:

"Father, do you see the container, pitcher, or whatever it is lying there, just to give an example?"

---

and incorrect insertion. It is, moreover, possible that the martyrs were arrested there, but were not from there. Some scholars maintain, then, that Carthage was actually Perpetua's hometown, which seems to fit the narrative of the <u>Passion</u> better. In either event, a gentlewoman of Thuburbo Minus would have been very familiar with Carthage, which for that area was the city. (For a presentation of the pro-Thuburbo case in English [and further discussion of what we know of Perpetua's life], see Harris & Gifford, <u>Acts</u> 2-7; for the anti-Thuburbo case, see Robinson, <u>Passion</u> 22-26.)

According to Roman custom, Perpetua may have been married as early as age eleven, but the text gives no information about her age at marriage, nor does it reveal anything about the nature of her marriage or about her husband, whose absence from the text is a puzzle. Explanations for his absence include: he was still a pagan and did not agree with Perpetua's conversion to Christianity and therefore did not see her while she was imprisoned; he was dead; he was away for some reason; the editor ignored her husband so as not to distract from the great actions of the martyrs and from the critical father/daughter relationship (Salisbury, <u>Passion</u> 8).

[7] The text actually includes a section written by the martyr Saturus and narrative and concluding remarks by the editor.

[8] In the Roman world, a newborn child would be placed at the feet of its father, who would then decide if the child would live or not. The father was the head of the family, and his authority was nearly absolute, although a family council (males only!) and public opinion restrained fathers from straying too far outside society's norms. A father's relationship with his daughter was important because daughters enabled the family to create political and social ties through marriage. Yet the evidence indicates that Roman fathers also often loved their daughters and forged special bonds of affection with them; the great rhetorician/politician Cicero's grief at the death of his daughter provides one example. The special relationship between Perpetua and her father, as the <u>Passion</u> will show, provides another. (Judith P. Hallett's <u>Fathers and Daughters in Roman Society</u> [Princeton University Press, 1984] provides a useful investigation, although it does not treat Perpetua and her father.)

He said:

"I do."

(2) And I said to him:

"Can you call it anything other than what it is?"

He said:

"No."

"Well, I cannot call myself anything but what I am, a Christian."

(3) This word so infuriated my father that he lunged at me as if he was going to pluck my eyes out. But he merely became angry and left, defeated along with his devilish arguments.[9] (4) I gave thanks to the Lord for the fact that my father stayed away for the next few days, and his absence helped me to recover. (5) In this space of a few days, we were baptized, and the Spirit told me that I should ask for nothing from the water except for endurance of the flesh.[10] After a few days, we were taken to jail. I became terrified

---

[9] This questioning clearly has elements of Socrates' interrogations of helpless victims in Plato's dialogues: the employment of every-day life to elucidate the most momentous issues, the concern with definition, the attempt to get at the underlying nature of things. For the ancients (and for many moderns), Socrates was the quintessential principled prisoner of conscience and a martyr to truth. It is not surprising that Perpetua's father reacted so violently, since the Socratic mode of her questioning suggested that she was the master and he the learner, and intimated that she was possessed of virtue that he had not yet grasped. It is worth noting that the historical Socrates irritated his share of interlocutors as well.

[10] Christian baptism is a ubiquitous theme in the Passion. As far as we can tell, Christian candidates of about 200 CE would disrobe – they were baptised naked – renounce Satan, and they were then anointed with oil. After entering the water, they would three times confess their faith, and after each confession, they would be immersed in the water. Then they would come out of the water and again be anointed and clothed. They would experience another anointing with the laying on of hands, and then they would exchange the kiss of peace with the congregation. The congregation would then celebrate with a Eucharist. One of our best sources for baptism in this period was Perpetua's fellow African, Tertullian, who in the years immediately preceding her martyrdom wrote an essay On Baptism (de baptismo) in which he explicitly relates baptism to martyrdom, "a second font...of blood" and asserts that martyrdom can take the place of baptism (16). Virtually every aspect of baptism just outlined will inform the imagery of the following pages.

because I had never experienced such darkness. (6) What a horrible day! The overcrowding made the heat unbearable...the guards and their extortion...and worst of all, concern for my baby tormented me there.[11] (7) Then Tertius and Pomponius, the blessed deacons who ministered to us, through bribery arranged to get us a few hours in a better part of the jail to help us refresh ourselves.[12] (8) Then they left the jail together to see to other business. But I nursed my baby, who had become weak from hunger. Since I was

---

[11] "Jail" is a better translation than the more common "prison," since they were used to confine people temporarily; the Romans did not sentence criminals to time in prison as a punishment as we do. Still, these supposedly temporary incarcerations could last for months, even years, and occasionally governors left people in jail to punish them, although they were not supposed to, yet another indication of how a governor could be virtually a law unto himself. (Wansink, Chained 28-33).

By any standard, Roman jails were awful. They resembled medieval dungeons more than modern jails and prisons, however horrible they can be. Perpetua's description of a dark, overcrowded, sweltering hole is typical of our sources. Jails tended to be underground and without sources of light and ventilation; they stank terribly, and prisoners often had difficulty even breathing. Jails almost never had cells, and all the prisoners would be lumped together in one room; male and female prisoners were often not segregated. Some ancient jails had two sections, a preferable outer section (presumably nearer to light and fresh air) and a more dismal and unwholesome inner section. In many of them, the prisoners were chained most of the time, and particularly at night. It is no surprise that such toxic conditions killed many prisoners. These dark, foul, claustrophobic, filthy holes also had a devastating effect on prisoners' psychological state. We must imagine Perpetua spending her incarceration in just such a wretched environment. (Wansink, Chained 33-95, provides the most useful treatment of conditions in Roman jails.)

[12] Bribery was common and expected among the Romans, especially among soldiers and other agents of the state. Guards were no different, and many of them clearly expected to supplement their incomes by extorting money from the relatives and friends of prisoners. Guards had an immense amount of control over prisoners and were in a position to abuse them physically; they were often brutal. One of the Carthaginian martyrs, Secundulus, was killed with a sword while still in jail (section 14.2); he may have been executed, but he may also have been murdered by the guards under some pretext or other. Relatives and friends were essential to mitigating the horrors of Roman jails, however slightly, and the early Christians were particularly dutiful about visiting and tending to their own. (On the critical roles that guards and visitors played for the incarcerated, again see Wansink, Chained 41-95.)

so worried about him, I spoke to my mother about him, comforted my brother, and entrusted my baby to them. I was falling apart because I saw how they were falling apart out of concern for me. (9) I endured these sorts of anxieties for many days. But then I obtained permission for my baby to stay with me in jail, and at once I was revitalized and was freed from my burdensome anxiety for him. Suddenly, the jail became a palace in my eyes, so that I preferred to be there rather than anywhere else.

4. Then my brother said to me:[13]

"Revered sister, now you have great honor, so much honor that you could request a vision to show you whether you will suffer or be released."[14]

(2) And because I knew that I could speak about these things with the Lord, whose wonderful blessings I had experienced, I confidently promised him that I would, saying:

"I will report to you tomorrow."

---

[13] Since the early Christians often called each other brother and sister, it is at times difficult to know for certain when in this text these words refer to biological siblings and when to brothers and sisters in Christ. The fact that Perpetua designates Dinocrates her "brother in the flesh" (7.5) suggests blood kinship, however, and that the reader should assume that persons designated only as brothers and sisters are fellow Christians, and not biological kin, unless some specific language or the context indicates otherwise.

[14] The Latin for "Revered sister" is *Domina soror*. *Domina* means "Lady," in the sense of "Lord and Lady," and is the feminine of the word that this and other Christian Latin texts use to refer to "the Lord," that is, God. *Dominus* meant "master" and quite naturally came to be applied to the emperors. (The word "mistress," as the feminine equivalent of "master," once provided a serviceable translation for *domina*, but "mistress" has taken on a different meaning in contemporary English). That Perpetua would now be addressed in this way indicates the great authority and power those who continued to confess their faith in the face of death enjoyed in early Christianity; they were even elevated above the actual hierarchy of the Church. Persons who were persecuted for Jesus gained so much authority and reverence that they did not even need to be ordained to become presbyters (Hall, "Women" 303). The use of *domina* may also suggest that Perpetua's husband is dead and that she is "of independent standing" (Hall, "Women" 318), but this is far from certain.

So I asked for a vision, and this is what was shown to me.[15] (3) I saw a bronze ladder of remarkable height that reached all the way to heaven, but it was so narrow that only one person at a time could climb it. Attached to the ladder's sides were all types of iron weapons. The swords, lances, hooks, daggers, and javelins were positioned so that those who climbed carelessly or without concentrating their gaze upwards would be mangled, and their flesh would cling to the iron weapons. [16] (4) And lying under the ladder was an enormous serpent who would ambush and terrify those trying to climb, intent on preventing them from ascending.[17] (5) Nevertheless Saturus climbed up first.

---

[15] Dreams and visions were a large part of both pagan and early Christian culture. In the Romans' national epic, the Aeneid, for example, the hero Aeneas receives instructions and views of the future in dreams and visions. In Matthew's account of the Nativity, to give a Christian example, an angel passes God's instructions to Joseph in dreams. Ancient interpretations of what dreams were and what they meant were different from those today. Ancient Christians and pagans tended to believe that dreams and visions were divinely inspired. As religious experiences entailing contact with God (Christians) or a god (pagans), dreams could be viewed as even more significant than experiences in the real world, and they were believed to foretell the future and provide guidance. It is not surprising, then, that both Perpetua and Saturus recorded their dreams and that the editor of the Passion thought they were worth preserving. Perpetua was convinced that she was blessed and had the privilege of asking for a vision because being arrested was a sign that one had been selected to be a martyr. Modern psychoanalytic interpretations of these dreams, on the other hand, have attempted to gain understanding of unconscious conflicts in Perpetua's and Saturus' minds. (Salisbury, Passion 92-95, 98)

 The analysis of dreams in the Roman Empire was a full-blown pseudo-science. The most useful surviving expression of the discipline is The Interpretation of Dreams (oneirocritica) by Artemidorus, who lived in the second century CE, that is, in the century leading up to Perpetua's death. Artemidorus provides a user-friendly, systematic, practical guidebook for the interpretation of dreams; it is no theoretical work. For us, it is a gold mine of information on what the Greeks and Romans made of the bizarre images and occurrences in their dreams; some of this information can help us understand Perpetua's visions, or at least the pagan background to the interpretation of dreams of which she must have been aware. Robert J. White's English translation of Artemidorus includes helpful commentary and a thematic index (The Interpretation of Dreams by Artemidorus; Noyes Press, 1975).

(He wasn't there when we were arrested but turned himself in later, because he was the one who had instructed us.) (6) When he reached the top of the ladder, he turned around and said to me:

"Perpetua, I am waiting for you, but make sure that the serpent does not bite you."

And I said:

"It will not harm me, in the name of Jesus Christ."

(7) As if it was afraid of me, the serpent slowly slithered

---

[16] This ladder extending to heaven suggests Jacob's ladder from the book of Genesis (28:12): "And he dreamed that there was a ladder set up on the earth, and the top of it reached to heaven; and behold, the angels of God were ascending and descending on it!" But Perpetua also drew on a rich pagan heritage which could have contributed to this vision; Artemidorus says that a ladder symbolizes travel, progress, and danger – all applicable to Perpetua's vision (2.42). Also, the ladder was made out of bronze, a relatively malleable metal, and lined with weapons of iron, which is much harder and stronger than bronze. Perpetua may be apprehensive that her salvation, symbolized by the ladder, is not as strong as the impediments to her salvation, symbolized by the weapons framing the ladder.

[17] In both the Old and New Testaments, reptiles refer to Satan. Perhaps the most famous and relevant example is from the book of Revelation (12.3-9): "And another portent appeared in heaven; behold, a great red dragon, with seven heads and ten horns, and seven diadems upon his heads. His tail swept down a third of the stars of heaven, and cast them to the earth. And the dragon stood before the woman who was about to bear a child, that he might devour her child when she brought it forth; she brought forth a male child, one who is to rule all the nations with a rod of iron, but her child was caught up to God and to his throne, and the woman fled into the wilderness, where she has a place prepared by God, in which to be nourished for one thousand two hundred and sixty days. Now war arose in heaven, Michael and his angels fighting against the dragon; and the dragon and his angels fought, but they were defeated and there was no longer any place for them in heaven. And the great dragon was thrown down, that ancient serpent, who is called the Devil and Satan, the deceiver of the whole world – he was thrown down to the earth, and his angels were thrown down with him."

According to Artemidorus, serpents can signify a great variety of things, and the particulars of the dream and of the dreamer's situation multiply the possibilities (2.13 , 4.67, 4. 68, 4. 79). Among the possibilities of greatest interest for Perpetua's vision: kings, illness, an enemy (the way the serpent behaves in the dream is how the enemy will behave in real life); venomous creatures represent powerful men (4.56); Perpetua's has just rejected her father and will soon defy the emperor's representative (and thus the emperor) by refusing to abandon her faith.

its head out from under the ladder. And as if I was stepping on the first rung of the ladder, I trod on the serpent's head and climbed.[18] (8) And I saw a vast garden, and in the middle of it sat a tall, grey-haired man wearing the clothes of a shepherd, and he was milking sheep. Standing around him were many thousands of people dressed in white.[19] (9) He lifted his head, gazed at me and said:

"It is good that you have come, my child."

And he called to me, and from the curd he had milked, he

---

[18] Perpetua's trampling the head of the serpent recalls God's declaration to the serpent in the Garden of Eden after it had tempted Adam and Eve (Gen 3:14-15): "Because you have done this, cursed are you above all cattle, and above all wild animals; upon your belly you shall go, and dust you shall eat all the days of your life. I will put enmity between you and the woman, and between your seed and her seed; he shall bruise your head, and you shall bruise his heel." Perpetua's action in the dream, then, foretells her defeat of Satan.

[19] The garden that Perpetua arrives at could be derived from the second-century Apocalypse of St. Peter in which Peter saw heaven as a garden with trees, fruits, and sweet smells. It could also be a reflection of the Garden of Eden seen in Genesis 2:8-9: "And the Lord God planted a garden in Eden, in the east; and there he put the man whom he had formed. And out of the ground the Lord God made to grow every tree that is pleasant to the sight and good for food, the tree of life also in the midst of the garden, and the tree of the knowledge of good and evil." The old shepherd is clearly God, as this image of the Good Shepherd was prevalent in the early church, and Perpetua very likely knew of the Shepherd of Hermas, a late-first, early-second-century apocalyptic work, in part of which a shepherd guides a dreamer. Both texts portray the shepherd as young and handsome. (See Robinson, Acts 26-43, for a comprehensive discussion of the influence of the Apocalypse of St. Peter and Shepherd of Hermas on the visions in Perpetua's Passion.) Salisbury, Passion 102-103, argues that Perpetua is combining these images of a young shepherd with that of her father; both the shepherd and her father are described as grey-haired. A heavenly father, then, will replace the wordly father that Perpetua rejected. The thousands of people dressed in white reflect John's vision in Revelation (7:9-12), which may have informed other elements of Perpetua's visions as well: "After this I looked, and behold, a great multitude which no man could number, from every nation, from all tribes and peoples and tongues, standing before the throne and before the Lamb, clothed in white robes, with palm branches in their hands, and crying out with a loud voice, 'Salvation belongs to our God who sits upon the throne, and to the Lamb!' And all the angels stood round the throne and round the elders and the four living creatures, and they fell on their faces before the throne and worshiped God, saying, 'Amen! Blessing and glory and wisdom and thanksgiving and honor and power and might be to our God for ever and ever! Amen!'"

gave me more or less a morsel. I took it into my cupped hands and ate it, and all together those standing around said:

"Amen."[20]

(10) At the sound of that word I awoke, still tasting something sweet.[21] At once I told my brother. We understood that I would suffer, and from that point, we ceased to have hope in this world.

5. After a few days, a rumor spread that we would have our hearing. And so, overwhelmed by worry, my father arrived from town, and he came to dissuade me, saying:

(2) "My daughter, have pity on my grey hair; have pity on your father, if I am worthy to be called father by you, if with these hands of mine I have raised you to this prime of life, if I have placed you before your brothers. Do not leave me in disgrace! (3) Think of your brothers; think of your mother and your aunt; think of your son, who will not be able to live without you. (4) Stop being so stubborn. Don't you see that you are going to ruin us all? For none of us will be able to speak freely if this awful thing happens to you."

(5) My father kept saying such things, just as you would expect a devoted father to, and kissing my hands he threw

---

[20] This portion of her vision is obviously reminiscent of the ritual of the Eucharist. The word translated as "curd" is *caseus*, the Latin word for "cheese." Patricia Cox Miller notes that Christians in Carthage ate cheese in addition to the bread and wine of Communion, but the cupping of Perpetua's hands may suggest that it was still in a semi-solid or even liquid state, thus "curds" (our choice) or "milk" (the most common translation of the word but a looser one; milk was also part of the Carthaginian eucharistic meal, however). When mixed with honey, milk symbolized (and still does) the Promised Land and the nourishment of Christ. Miller also notes that this brings to mind the biblical idea of the land of milk and honey and references to milk as the drink of eternity in other African martyrdoms ("The Devil's Gateway: An Eros of Difference in the Dreams of Perpetua," Dreaming 2.1 [1992] 45-63).

[21] This could be an allusion to the bread consumed at the Eucharist, or it might just be proof that the vision was not merely imagined, but divinely inspired, and hence has tangible remnants. Or both.

himself at my feet. Weeping, he called me not "daughter," but "Lady."[22] (6) And I grieved over my father's misfortune, since he alone of all my family would not rejoice in my suffering.[23] And I comforted him, saying:

"What happens at the hearing will be what God wants. For you need to understand that we are created not in our own power, but in God's."

And heartbroken he left me.

6. While we were eating breakfast one day, we were suddenly taken away to the forum for our hearing. After we got there, the news sped through the adjacent neighborhoods, and an immense crowd gathered. (2) We climbed the platform. The other prisoners confessed. Then it was my turn. My father suddenly appeared with my son and dragged me from the steps, saying:

"Perform the sacrifice![24] Pity your baby!"

(3) And the governor, Hilarianus, who had assumed the powers of that office when Minucius Timinianus died,[25] said:

"Show mercy on your father's grey hair; show mercy on your infant son. Perform the sacrifice for the well-being of the emperors."

(4) And I answered:

"I will not."

Hiliarianus asked:

---

[22] The Latin: *Domina* (on the import of the word, see note on section 4.1 above). In a remarkable inversion of the normal Roman family structure, Perpetua's father appeals to her as a slave to a master, or a subject to his lord.

[23] It is difficult to know precisely what to make of Perpetua's assertion. It may be that the rest of her family is pagan like her father but unlike him detests her for her choice and so is eager to see her suffer. Or, it could be that the rest of her family is Christian and so takes pride in her faithfulness and rejoices that she will be joining God in Paradise; we know that one of her brothers, after all, was a catechumen. The absence of her husband is curious, but even more puzzling is that Perpetua says not a word about him or where he might be. See note to section 2.3.

"Are you a Christian?"

I replied:

"I am a Christian."[26]

(5) But when my father kept on trying to shake my resolve, Hilarianus ordered him to be knocked down and beaten with a rod.[27] My father's affliction caused me as much

---

[24] Sacrifice, making offerings, and prayer were among the principal ways pagans interacted with and influenced their gods (see the Introduction for a discussion of festivals). In return for sacrifices and offerings (animals might be slain, wine might be poured onto the ground, and the like), pagans anticipated that the gods would favor them and grant specific requests. Sacrifice to the emperor's *genius* and for his health made perfect sense; the emperor's unparalleled, almost divine, power merited divine honors, and the prosperity of the entire empire was entwined with that of the emperor. Sacrifice to the emperor, who embodied Rome's power and authority, also had elements of a kind of loyalty oath. Pliny compelled those denounced to him as Christians to offer incense and wine as an identification test, since Christians are not able to sacrifice. Already with Pliny, though, there was an inclination to coerce these stubborn, impudent people to submit to Rome's authority. It is not surprising that the compulsory sacrifice evolved into an attempt to break the Christians, to make them publically deny their faith, to conform. (For the imperial cult, see especially S. R. F. Price, Rituals and Power: The Roman Imperial Cult in Asia Minor [Cambridge University Press, 1984].)

[25] James Rives and others have plausibly identified this Hilarianus with P. Aelius Hilarianus, who served as governor in Spain as well (Rives, "Persecution," 1-10; see, too, Barnes, Tertullian 163). If this identification is correct, "we can say a fair amount about the persecutor of Perpetua. His family was probably of Greek origin and could not have held Roman citizenship for more than two or three generations before him...When we first have evidence for our Hilarianus, he is in the upper echelons of the imperial bureaucracy, but it is likely that he had worked his way up...Hilarianus thus appears as an ambitious and successful man, who rose from a relatively modest backgound to the highest levels of Roman government and society. It is not surprising that such a man would have had little sympathy for a young woman of good family who had abandoned her place in society in order to join a bizarre and potentially dangerous sect."(9-10)

Evidently Hilarianus was filling in as a substitute governor for the deceased Timinianus. Still, the text indicates that he had the *ius gladii*, the power of life and death, over the residents of the province.

[26] The brevity and even the precise words in the martyrs' trial resemble those of the Scillitan martyrs (see Appendix 2); the encounter with Perpetua's father, however, is unlike anything in the Scillitan account.

[27] Hilarianus may be trying to press Perpetua to relent by abusing her father. Or he may simply be venting his anger at these unrepentant Christians. And he may be furious with Perpetua's father for losing control of his daughter and for what must have appeared to Hilarianus as a humiliating display of unnatural male subservience to a woman.

pain as if it had been I who was beaten, and so I grieved over his pitiful old age. (6) Then Hilarianus condemned us all and sentenced us to the beasts.[28] We returned to jail cheerfully.[29] (7) Since my baby had gotten used to feeding from my breasts and staying with me in the jail, I immediately sent the deacon Pomponius to my father to ask for the baby. But my father refused to send him. (8) Yet God willed that my son no longer desire to feed at my breasts and that they cease to swell with milk. And so I ceased to be tormented by worry about my child or by pain in my breasts.

7. A few days later, while we were all praying together, I suddenly called out in the middle of our prayer and said the name:

"Dinocrates."

This astonished me, since the name had never occurred to me until that moment. It pained me to remember his tragedy. (2) But at once I recognized that I was worthy to pray for him and that I ought to do so.[30] And so I began to pray for him a great deal and to lament over him to the Lord. (3) That night I had the following vision. (4) I saw Dinocrates emerge from a shadowy place, where there were

---

[28] Generally, there were three categories of corporal punishment for criminals: *ad gladium, ad ludum,* and *ad bestias.* Those sentenced *ad gladium* were doomed to death by the sword. Only men were condemned *ad ludum,* that is, to gladiatorial training, which was known to be a lesser punishment since death was far from certain at the contests in the arena. Criminals pitted against the fierce animals of the arena, or *ad bestias,* would die.

[29] Perpetua describes the martyrs as "cheerful" or "happy" here because martyrs in early Christianity considered themselves privileged, and they were convinced that they would be greatly rewarded in heaven. See the Introduction, pages 56-57

[30] Since it was common for Christians in the early Church to break out in prophetic utterances during prayer, it was natural for Perpetua to see God's hand in her exclamation. And because prophecy was a privilege, Perpetua took her utterance as a sign that praying for her brother might effect a change in his condition (Salisbury, <u>Passion</u> 104-05).

also many others. He was hot and thirsty, his clothes were filthy and his face pale. And on his face was the sore he had when he died. (5) Dinocrates was my brother in the flesh who had died in his seventh year of an illness that so horribly disfigured his face with lesions that his death revolted everyone.[31] (6) It was for him, then, that I prayed. But in my vision, between him and me there was a gulf so great that we could not approach each other.[32] (7) On Dinocrates' side, there was a pool full of water whose rim was higher than the boy's height. He kept stretching himself up to try to drink. (8) I was saddened because, even though the pool had water, he could not reach it to drink since the rim was too high for him. (9) I awoke, and I realized that my brother was struggling. But I was confident that I could relieve his suffering. And I prayed for him every day until we were transferred to the military jail. They moved us there because we were going to fight in the camp games for Geta Caesar's

---

[31] A careful storyteller would have told us who Dinocrates was earlier; the sequence in this part of Perpetua's narrative is peculiar, even a bit confusing. This can be taken, however, as evidence that we are dealing with an authentic prison diary, not a carefully crafted and edited literary composition.

[32] This great gulf and Dinocrates' thirst and sore seem inspired by one of Jesus' parables (Luke 16:19-26): "There was a rich man, who was clothed in purple and fine linen and who feasted sumptuously every day. And at his gate lay a poor man named Lazarus, full of sores, who desired to be fed with what fell from the rich man's table; moreover the dogs came and licked his sores. The poor man died and was carried by the angels to Abraham's bosom. The rich man also died and was buried; and in Hades, being in torment, he lifted up his eyes, and saw Abraham far off and Lazarus in his bosom. And he called out, 'Father Abraham, have mercy upon me, and send Lazarus to dip the end of his finger in water and cool my tongue; for I am in anguish in this flame.' But Abraham said, 'Son, remember that you in your lifetime received your good things, and Lazarus in like manner evil things; but now he is comforted, and you are in anguish. And besides all this, between us and you a great chasm has been fixed, in order that those who would pass from here to you may not be able, and none may cross from there to us.'"

birthday.[33] (10) And I prayed for Dinocrates day and night, moaning and weeping that my wish for him be granted.

8. On the day they kept us in chains, I had another vision. I saw the same place where I had before seen Dinocrates, but he was well-dressed and clean and was refreshing himself. Where the sore used to be, I saw a scar. (2) The rim of the pool I had seen in my earlier vision was lowered to his waist, and Dinocrates kept drawing water from it without pause. (3) Above the rim was a golden cup, full of water. Dinocrates approached the cup and began to drink from it, and the cup never ran out of water.[34] (4) And

---

[33] In this translation, the Latin *munus* (singular)/*munera* (plural) is rendered "games" or "contest." The *munus* followed a particular sequence over the course of a few days: mornings were reserved for animal hunts; noontime for executions, athletic contests, ballets, and comedy; and later in the day for gladiatorial combats.

Geta was the second son of Lucius Septimius Severus, the emperor of Rome from 197-211 CE. The Historia Augusta, an often unreliable fourth-century collection of biographies of emperors, claims that Septimius Severus forbade conversion to Judaism and Christianity ("Iudaeos fieri vetuit. idem sanxit de Christianis" [Severus 17.1]). Some believe that this supposed decree was the catalyst for the persecution of Perpetua and her friends and for an outbreak of persecution in Alexandria of Egypt (Carthage's rival for second city of the Roman Empire); see, for example, W. H. C. Frend, "A Severan Persecution? Evidence of the Historia Augusta," in Forma Futuri: Studi in Onore del Cardinale Michele Pellegrino (1975) 470-489. This decree is most likely unhistorical, however, as Timothy Barnes, among others, has shown (Early Christianity 40-41). The story of Perpetua and her friends actually provides evidence against the historicity of the edict: the Carthaginian martyrs were clearly punished for being Christians, not for becoming Christians; this edict would also have been pointless unless being a Christian had been legalized, but events in Carthage show clearly that being a Christian was as illegal as ever. As usual, the cause of the outbreak of persecution is not to be found in the palace in Rome, but in the provinces.

[34] Perpetua's vision indicates that her intercessory prayers have saved Dinocrates. He is portrayed as clean, well-dressed, and refreshed. Also, the cancer on his face had healed leaving only a scar. Artemidorus claims that a scar symbolizes the end of every care and that a drinking bowl above a pool symbolizes great safety. From a Christian perspective, the pool that Dinocrates now plays in brings to mind the scriptural image of the healing of the paralytic by the side of the pool at Bethesda (John 5:2-9): "Now there is in Jerusalem by the Sheep Gate a pool, in Hebrew called Beth-zatha, which has five porticoes. In these lay a multitude of invalids, blind, lame, paralyzed. One man was there, who had been ill for thirty-eight

when he had quenched his thirst, he began to play joyfully like a child. Then I awoke. I understood that he had been freed from his punishment.[35]

years. When Jesus saw him and knew that he had been lying there a long time, he said to him, 'Do you want to be healed?' The sick man answered him, 'Sir, I have no man to put me into the pool when the water is troubled, and while I am going another steps down before me.' Jesus said to him, 'Rise, take up your pallet, and walk.' And at once the man was healed, and he took up his pallet and walked."

[35] The word translated as "punishment" is *poena*. Translators tend to render the work as "suffering," or something of that sort. Though *poena* certainly entails suffering, its primary meaning is clear. What, precisely, Perpetua has accomplished is uncertain. If, in fact, Perpetua's description of the great gulf between her and her brother refers to the gulf between heaven and hell (an interpretation strengthened by the correspondences between Perpetua's vision and the parable quoted above), the passage would seem to suggest that Perpetua thought that she had rescued her brother from hell. Or has she seen him in purgatory? Purgatory did not become Roman Catholic doctrine until the Middle Ages (even the Latin term *purgatorium* is medieval), but the idea of a stage after death in which souls could be purged of sin is ancient. This passage concerning Dinocrates is as one of the earliest (if not the earliest) and most important indications of this belief among early Christians, and of the belief that the prayers of the living could aid the dead. If this is a vision of purgatory, then, Perpetua was a pioneer or, a pious Roman Catholic might maintain, she had a vision of a reality that was not revealed to the Church as doctrine until much later. (An accessible, comprehensive study of purgatory is Jacques Le Goff's The Birth of Purgatory [trans. Arthur Goldhammer; University of Chicago Press, 1994].) In any event, the vision provides a powerful confirmation of the belief in the power of prayer, especially martyrs' prayers.

Perpetua's vision also resonates with pagan imaginings of the Underworld. In Book 6 of his Aeneid, Vergil has Aeneas hear the weeping and wailing of children at its entrance: "Now voices crying loud were heard at once – /The souls of infants wailing. At the door/Of the sweet life they were to have no part in,/Torn from the breast, a black day took them off/And drowned them all in bitter death" (translation by Robert Fitzgerald [Vintage, 1981] 174). And when Aeneas meets Dido there, she bears the wounds that killed her in life, just like Dinocrates. Perpetua's vision most obviously evokes the myth of Tantalus. He chopped up his son Pelops and made a stew out of him. He served the stew to the gods, all of whom, except Demeter, recognized the revolting dish. They condemned him to eternal thirst and hunger in the Underworld (Pindar, Olympian Ode 1 [a poem composed to celebrate an athletic victory at the ancient Olympics]; Pindar, however, can scarcely bring himself to believe the story is true). When Odysseus visited the Underworld in Homer's Odyssey (Book 11), he saw Tantalus standing in a pool that would reach up to his chin. When Tantalus would try to drink, the waters would recede and dry up. Lush trees dangled their succulent fruits just above his head, but whenever he would reach up to pick the fruits, the wind would blow them out of his reach. It is worth

9. A few days later, a military adjutant named Pudens, who was in charge of the jail, began to honor us since he recognized that there was great power[36] in us. He allowed many people to visit us so that we and our visitors might console and restore each other. (2) Now when the day for our contest drew near, my father, consumed with sorrow, came to see me. He began to tear hair from his beard and throw it on the ground and to prostrate himself before me. He cursed his old age and uttered words that would move all creation. But I could only mourn for his miserable old age.

10. On the day before we were to fight, I had another vision. Pomponius the deacon came to the gate of the jail and fiercely knocked on it. (2) I went out to him and opened the gate. He was dressed in unbelted[37] white garments and wore elaborate sandals.[38] (3) And he said to me:

"Perpetua, we await you. Come."

Then he extended his hand to me, and we began to travel through harsh and winding lands. (4) With difficulty we at last arrived, panting, at the amphitheater, and Pomponius brought me into the middle of the arena and said to me:[39]

---

noting that Tantalus was being punished for his impiety. Odysseus' and Aeneas' visits to the Underworld were among the classic passages of ancient literature and so surely known to an educated Roman woman like Perpetua. Artemidorus asserts that thirst in a dream means a longing for something (1.66); elsewhere he states that a drinking cup represents life itself (1.74).

[36] This is the same word, *virtutem*, that was employed at the beginning of the <u>Passion</u> to describe the power or efficacy of the Holy Spirit; see the note to 1.3.

[37] The Latin translated as "unbelted" is *discincta*, meaning "unbound" or "not tied." During rituals Roman pagan priest would wear unbound garments since knots were ill-omened; they suggested restriction and convolution. The *flamen Dialis*, the priest dedicated to Jupiter (the Romans' most important god), could not have knots or bindings anywhere on his clothes.

[38] The inhabitants of Paradise in Perpetua's first vision were similarly dressed.

[39] Romans referred to the oval building that housed the games as an amphitheater; modern football stadiums are descendents of ancient amphitheaters. The arena,

"Do not be afraid. I am here with you, and I will share in your struggle."

Then he went away. (5) And I saw a huge, astonished crowd. Since I knew that I had been condemned to the beasts, I was surprised that none were set on me. (6) Instead, a vile Egyptian accompanied by seconds came out to battle me.[40] Handsome young men also came out, but to be my seconds and supporters. (7) I was then disrobed, and I became a man.[41] My supporters began to rub oil on me, as is the custom before athletic competitions.[42] I saw the Egyptian

---

derived from the Latin word *harena*, meaning "sand," designated the field, the central open area where the spectacles took place; it often consisted of a wooden flooring covered with sand where gladiators and others provided entertainment. The amphitheater at Carthage was constructed around 133-139 CE, and underwent an extensive renovation after 165. At 512 by 420 feet, it was an appropriately impressive structure for a city of Carthage's importance, seating roughly 30,000 spectators (on the amphitheater, see Bomgardner, Amphitheater 85-103).

[40] Shaw, "Perpetua," dismisses the nationality of the Egyptian as "a simple reflection of racism" (n. 62, p. 28). There seems to be a good deal more than that at play here, however, and the issue is significant because the Egyptian clearly represents the devil. This nationality was perhaps chosen because many of the Roman mystic cults at the time originated in the eastern regions, including Egypt. Emperor Septimus Severus gave the cult of the Egyptian god Serapis particular attention (Salisbury, Passion 20). It may be, then, that the choice of an Egpytian not only reflects other cults competing with Christianity for the attention and hearts of Roman pagans, but also the Roman authorities' fostering of those cults while oppressing the Christians. Perpetua would have been aware of Revelation's association of Christianity's Roman persecutors with the devil. For more discussion of some of these and of other possibilities, see Salisbury, Passion 110-111.

[41] Artemidorus is of little use here. He claims that if a woman who has a child and a husband dreams that she becomes a man (he does not address widows in the passage), she will end her life as a widow (1.50). On the transformation, see the Introduction, pp. 16-17.

[42] Athletes competing in Greco-Roman athletic festivals would in fact be oiled down before competing; only men participated, and they competed in the nude. Perpetua interprets her vision, then, in purely athletic terms, which fits the context perfectly and makes even more sense, considering that Christians often used athletic imagery and had been doing so since the time of the New Testament. The astonishing elements in this passage, then, can be viewed simply as reflecting the logistics and conventions of ancient athletic competition. It is no surprise, however, that they have received a good deal of scholarly attention, as readers have found in them depths of implicit meaning. Does Perpetua need to transform into a man since only men can achieve any kind of greatness

rolling in the dust on the other side of the arena. (8) And a man came, a man of such remarkable height that he was even taller than the top of the amphitheater. He wore an unbelted garment with two purple stripes down the middle of his chest and intricate shoes made of gold and silver.[43] The man was carrying a rod, just like a *lanista*, and a green branch with golden apples.[44] (9) He asked for silence and said:

---

in her patriarchal society? Isn't there something sexually suggestive about handsome young men rubbing down a young woman? In the ancient world, scented oils were in fact used as enhancements to sex. But the rubbing with oil and other aspects of this vision also suggest Christian baptism, a prominent motif throughout the text. Cathechumens (and it is worth recalling that in the Passion Perpetua starts out as a catechumen) would be immersed naked into a pool, and when they emerged from the water they were anointed with oil and donned white clothes. The ceremony was done before the congregation, making it a communal occasion but also something of a show. Does Perpetua need to become a man like Christ to emulate fully his Passion? Or does the transformation suggest, rather, that "there is neither male nor female" in Christ (Gal 3:28)? It is also not out of the question that Perpetua knew this passage from the apocryphal Gospel of Thomas (logion 14): "Simon Peter said to them, 'Mary should leave us, since women are not worthy of the Life.' Jesus said, 'See, I will lead her, so that I can make her male, so that she too can be transformed into a living spirit that resembles you males. For each woman who makes herself male will enter the Kingdom of Heaven.'" This would explain why she felt she needed to turn herself into a man: to gain salvation. (Artemidorus considered women dreaming of anointment auspicious, unless the dreamers were adulteresses [1.75].)

[43] The two stripes on the man's robe would have signified his status in ancient Rome. Roman peasants generally wore plain brownish tunics; the upper classes often wore tunics decorated with purple stripes. The fact that they could afford the purple dye was itself a sign of rank since it was quite expensive. The broadness of the stripes indicated rank. Senators wore the widest stripe. Below senators, but still near the pinnacle of Rome's social pyramid, were the *equites*, or knights, who wore a thinner purple stripe on their tunics.

[44] A *lanista* was actually an impresario/trainer who owned a troupe of gladiators. He would train his troupe and then rent them to an *editor*, or sponsor of the games, for spectacles. The late Oliver Reed portrayed a *lanista* (Proximo) in Ridley Scott's *Gladiator* (2000). Perpetua envisions no ordinary *lanista*, however. Hers is undoubtedly God. (In his To the Martyrs [ad martyres], Tertullian calls the Holy Spirit the trainer of martyrs [3.9-10], but he uses a term from Greek athletics, not from gladiatorial combat; in the Roman Empire, the worlds of athletics and gladiatorial combat were distinct. In Perpetua's vision, however, these worlds come together and blend.) A *lanista* would at times, in fact, carry a rod, symbol of his authority and power to punish his gladiators (gladiators

"If this Egyptian defeats her, he will kill her with his sword. But if she defeats him, she will receive the branch I am holding."

---

were slaves), but the rod of Perpetua's *lanista* may suggest Psalm 89:30-32: "If his children forsake my law and do not walk according to my ordinances, if they violate my statutes and do not keep my commandments, then I will punish their transgression with the rod and their iniquity with scourges," a passage of particular meaning to martyrs whose natural fear of their impending pain and death might cause them to falter; later in the Passion, moreover, the martyrs threaten the governor Hilarianus with God's punishment (18.8).

Normally, a contest winner would be given the "palm of victory," take a victory lap, present the branch to the spectators at the arena, and receive other prizes (Auguet, Cruelty 58). Perpetua receives a green branch with golden apples. Because she is victorious the apples cannot refer to the "Fall" in Genesis, according to Salisbury, Passion 111. But these apples could suggest that female Perpetua's faithfulness undoes female Eve's sin of disobedience; her victory is, in sense and very pointedly, the reverse of Eve's defeat. (It is worth noting that in the biblical narrative of the temptation of Eve, the fruit is not specified as an apple [Gen 3:3].) Any ancient reader would also be aware of the apple as a "symbol of woman and woman's love in the antique world." Salisbury notes that the apple represents "the highest prize of womanhood," as Aphrodite won a golden apple as the most beautiful goddess (112). This myth is more complicated, however. When the goddess Eris (Discord) is understandably not invited to the wedding of Thetis and Peleus (who will be the parents of Achilles, hero of the Iliad), she tosses into the party a golden apple inscribed with the words, "To the most beautiful." Aphrodite, goddess of love, Hera, queen of the gods, and Athena, a warrior goddess, each assumes that the apple must be for her. To settle who is the most beautiful and gets the golden apple, they ask the Trojan Paris to judge a beauty contest among them. All three bribe him, naturally, and being a young man Paris chooses Aphrodite's bribe (sex) over Hera's (political power) and Athena's (military power). His prize is Helen, the most ravishing woman in the world. Unfortunately, she is already married to Menelaus, king of Sparta. Paris gets his girl, but Menelaus and a coalition of Greek kings destroy Troy to get Helen back. This apple, too, brings with it destruction. After the golden apple that destroyed Troy, the golden apples of Greek mythology were those of the Hesperides (Daughters of Night). The three daughers inhabited a garden on the western fringes of the world, where they guarded a tree of golden apples with the help of a serpent named Ladon. Earth had given the tree to Hera as a wedding gift when she married Zeus. One of Hercules' twelve labors was to fetch the apples. In one version of the myth, he killed the serpent and took the apples. In another, he had Atlas fetch them for him, while he supported the heavens on his shoulders. Heracles' task, like much of his twelve labors, is (and was) taken to be an attempt to conquer death; the apples, then, were a kind of fruit of life. (For a more complete discussion of the symbolism in this vision, see Salisbury, Passion 106-112, who expands on the apple's associations with love and sex in the Greco-Roman world.)

(10) Then he stepped back. The Egyptian and I closed in on each other and began to throw punches.[45] He tried to grab my feet, but I countered by kicking him in the face with my heels. (11) Then I rose up into the air, as if floating, and I began to pound him. Then, when I realized there was a pause, I interlocked my fingers, and with my joined hands I gripped his head. He fell face-forward, and I trampled his head.[46] (12) The crowd began to cheer, and my aides sang psalms. I approached the *lanista* and received the branch. (13) He kissed me and said to me:

"My daughter, peace be with you."

I began to walk in glory towards the Gate of Life,[47] and I awoke. (14) I understood, then, that I was not going to fight against beasts, but against the devil. And I knew that I would defeat him. (15) That is what I did up to the day before the contest. As for what happened during the actual contest, anyone who wishes may write about it.

So ends Perpetua's part of the narrative; the editor takes over briefly.

---

[45] The battle Perpetua describes most closely resembles the pankration, a combat sport that could best be characterized as part boxing, part wrestling, and part judo. The rules allowed for wrestling, hitting, and kicking; indeed, only gouging in the body's most tender organs seems to have been prohibited. The contest was part of all of the Greco-Roman world's most prestigious athletic festivals, including the Olympics. It is worth recalling that these festivals, though they would to us most resemble track meets or events like the modern Olympics, were, at heart, religious observances honoring the pagan gods.

[46] This is a reference to the promise made to Eve in the Garden of Eden, that her heel would crush the head of the snake: "I will put enmity between you and the woman, and between your seed and her seed; he shall bruise your heel, and you shall bruise his head." (Gen 3:15)

[47] In Latin, the *Porta Sanavivaria*, through which successful, or at least, surviving, gladiators exited the arena; a different gate, the *Porta Libitinensis*, was used for those less fortunate.

11. In his own hand, the blessed Saturus also wrote down and made known his vision.

Next comes Saturus' description of his vision.[48]

(2) We had died and left the flesh, and four angels began to carry us towards the east, although their hands did not actually touch us. (3) However, we did not move lying on our backs, facing up, but as if we were climbing a gentle slope. (4) Once we were free of the world, we saw a brilliant light, and I said to Perpetua (who was at my side):

"This is what the Lord promised us. We have obtained his promise."

(5) And while the four angels were carrying us, a vast open space appeared to us; it was just like a cultivated garden with rose bushes and every kind of flower. (6) The trees in the garden were as tall as cypresses, and their leaves were falling continuously. (7) There were another four angels in the garden, more splendid than the four who carried us. And when they saw us, they honored us, and with admiration they said to the other angels:

"Behold, here they are! Here they are!"

And the four angels who were carrying us became afraid and put us down. (8) We then walked by a broad path towards a stadium. (9) There we found Jocundus,

---

[48] Some scholars wonder if the description of Saturus' vision is authentic. Shaw suggests: "But this vision is unlike Perpetua's not only in its language and its construction, but in its impersonal bent, its concern with theological interpretation and ecclesiastical hierarchy (underwritten as a template of divine order), a cast of new male characters, and a 'reread' Perpetua..." ("Perpetua" 31). Shaw then concludes that "there must be strong doubt that the account, as it stands, is indeed 'by him and in his own hand'" (32). We cannot rule out the possibility that Saturus' vision was reworked. The elements that Shaw finds suspicious, however, make perfect sense coming from an educated Christian man immersed in the life, controversies, and theological concerns of Carthage's Christian community.

Saturninus, and Artaxius, who were burned alive in the same persecution, and Quintus too, who had also died, but in jail. We asked them where they had been. (10) But the other angels said to us:

"First come, come in, and greet the Lord."

12. And we approached a place whose walls seemed to be made of light. Another four angels were standing in front of the place's gate, and as we entered they dressed us in white robes. (2) And when we had entered, we heard a chorus continuously chanting:

"Holy, Holy, Holy." [49]

(3) Then we saw someone sitting there, who appeared to be an old man. His hair was white, but his face was young, and we could not see his feet. (4) There were four elders on his right and on his left, and several other elders were standing behind him. (5) Full of wonder, we entered and stood before a throne. Then four angels picked us up, we kissed him, and with his hand he touched our faces. (6) And the rest of the elders said to us:

"Let us stand."

So we stood and gave the kiss of peace. And the elders said to us:

"Go and play."

(7) I said to Perpetua:

"You have what you want."

She answered me:

"Thanks be to God! For I am more joyful now in this place than I was in the flesh."

---

[49] Revelation 4:8: "And the four living creatures, each of them with six wings, are full of eyes all round and within, and day and night they never cease to sing, 'Holy, holy, holy, is the Lord God Almighty, who was and is and is to come!'" This passage describes Revelation's vision of heaven.

13. When we went out, we saw in front of the gates the bishop Optatus over to the right and the learned presbyter Aspasius over to the left, divided and sad.[50] (2) They rushed to our feet and said:

"It is up to you to reconcile us, since you have gone away and left us in this state."[51]

(3) But we said to them:

"Aren't you our bishop and you our presbyter? How can you cast yourselves at our feet?"

We were deeply moved, and we embraced them. (4) Then Perpetua began to converse with them in Greek. We took them aside into the cultivated garden and brought them together under a rose arbor. (5) But while we were speaking with them, the angels said to them:

"Let them rest. If you two are quarrelling, it is up to you to settle the dispute."

(6) The angels' words disturbed them. Then they said to Optatus:

"Set your congregation straight. As it is, they come to you behaving like fans returning from the races arguing

---

[50] For the ancient Christians, a bishop was the leader or pastor of the church; he was also considered the head of the presbyters. Presbyters oversaw community affairs. The text does not identify the nature of the dispute between Optatus and Apasius. Many of Tertullian's writings reflect the vehemence of some of the doctrinal debates of the day, and not just about Montanism. These debates would affect the administration of the congregations and have an impact on the life of the Christians as a community.

[51] Optatus and Aspasius appeal to Perpetua and Saturus to arbitrate their dispute. This indicates that because of their martyrdom, Perpetua and Saturus are in a position of authority over the church leaders. "It is well known that in early Christianity, martyrs awaiting death could exercise and manifest extraordinary power" (Klawiter, "Role" 254). Klawiter notes that those imprisoned for Christianity were seen to have the "power of the keys," or the power to confess sins, and that by 199 CE, a man who had been imprisoned as a Christian could automatically claim the title of presbyter upon his release (256).

about the teams."[52]

(7) And it looked to us as though they wanted to close the gates. (8) Then we began to recognize many of our brothers there, and martyrs as well. All of us were nourished by an indescribable odor that satisfied us. Then I awoke, rejoicing.

Here the editor takes over the narrative again.

14. Above are the glorious visions of the blessed martyrs Saturus and Perpetua, which they wrote down themselves. (2) But God summoned Secundulus from this world earlier than the other martyrs, while he was still in jail. And so God's grace saw to it that he avoided the beasts. Nevertheless his flesh knew the sword, although his soul most certainly did not.[53]

15. As for Felicity, the Lord's grace touched her as well, in the following way. (2) Already pregnant when they arrested her, she was now in her eighth month when the day scheduled for the spectacle was approaching. The timing deeply saddened her, since it looked as though her pregnancy would postpone her martyrdom – it was against the law for pregnant women to be brought out for execution – and so her holy, innocent blood would be shed not with her fellow martyrs, but later, in the company of com-

---

[52] Chariot racing was immensely popular, and its fans were notorious for their passion. Roman chariot racing was organized by "factions" (*factiones*), each of which consisted of the teams of horses (four per chariot), the charioteers, the stables (grooms, etc.), the owners, and the fans. The competing factions were identified by color: red, white, blue, and green. Most Romans (including some emperors) were adherents of one faction/color or another. To get an idea of a Roman fan's investment in his faction, one must imagine the most enthusiastic modern-day soccer aficionado.

[53] See note to section 3.7. Appendix 3 provides a chart outlining when and precisely how each martyr died.

mon criminals. (3) Her fellow martyrs were also deeply saddened at the prospect of leaving behind so outstanding a companion to travel alone the path of a shared hope. (4) And so with one, united groan, they poured forth a prayer to the Lord two days before the contest. (5) As soon as they had finished the prayer, Felicity went into labor. As you would expect with the difficulty of premature labor, Felicity endured considerable pain in giving birth. So one of the guards said to her:

"You are in so much pain now; what will you do when you are thrown to the beasts for whom you expressed so much contempt when you refused to sacrifice?"

(6) And she answered:

"What I suffer now, I suffer alone. But in the arena another will be in me, and that one will suffer on my behalf, since I am going to suffer on his."[54]

(7) Under these circumstances she gave birth to a girl, and a certain sister raised her as her own daughter.

16. Therefore, since the Holy Spirit has permitted, and by permitting has willed, that the sequence of events be written down, even though I am unworthy to add to such a glorious story, I shall carry out the blessed Perpetua's command, or more correctly, her dying request, adding another example of her steadfastness and of the loftiness of her soul. (2) The tribune began to restrict the martyrs' movements more severely, since the warnings of some ridiculous people

---

[54] Felicity may mean that the Holy Spirit will be inside of her, suffering for her when she faces the beasts. She may have Jesus in mind, whose Passion associated him in particular with suffering in the Christian imagination. If asked precisely to whom she was referring (or even if asked to specify a person of the Trinity), she may have simply answered, "God." In fact, the martyrs believed that the Holy Spirit was already with them. "Perpetua, Saturus, and Felicity had already felt the hand of God and the presence of the Spirit in preparing them for the ordeal that was to come the next day" (Salisbury, Passion 117).

had made him afraid that the martyrs would be spirited out of the jail by some sort of magical spell.[55] So Perpetua said to his face:

(3) "Why won't you permit us to maintain our health? Aren't we the most prized of the condemned, indeed, Caesar's own, since we are to fight on his birthday? Won't your position be enhanced, if on that day we are presented in better health?"

(4) The tribune became horrified, and his face turned red. So he ordered them to be treated more humanely and even allowed her brothers and others to visit them and comfort each other. By then the adjutant of the jail was also a believer.

17. On the day before the contest, when they were having their "last meal" as best they could, although they actually celebrated an *agape*, with their usual steadfastness they hurled words at the crowd, threatening them with God's judgment, presenting as proof[56] their joy at their own suffering, and mocking the curiosity of those who had gathered to see the martyrs.[57] (2) Saturus said:

"Isn't tomorrow enough for you? Why do you so delight

---

[55] The ancient world was full of gods, spirits, and supernatural forces. Magic was a way to control them. It garnered disapproval and even legislation prohibiting it since magic usurped the natural order of things, in which the gods are in control, and since it could be exercised outside of the supervision of the state (publicly) and of free, adult males (privately). Our sources seem to indicate that most ancient Greeks or Romans believed in some, if not most, elements of magic. It was often employed to injure or to force people to do something against their will. It was consequently feared. Pagans would be inclined to view the miracles of the New Testament as the result of magical spells. (In Jesus the Magician [Harper & Row, 1978], Morton Smith argues that Jesus would have been perceived first and foremost as a magician, and that this perception was, for many, a significant element of his appeal; see, too, Dickie, Magic 133-143.)

[56] Proof, evidently, of the correctness of their Christian faith. Only someone certain that a great reward awaited would be willing to endure joyfully the horrors of the arena.

in looking at what you hate? Today our friends...tomorrow our enemies. But take careful note of our faces, so that you will recognize us on that day."

And so everyone went away astonished, and many of them believed.

18. Dawn broke on the day of their victory. Elated, they marched from the jail to the amphitheater, as if they were marching to heaven; their faces were composed, and if they trembled at all, it was with joy, not fear. (2) Perpetua followed, her face radiant and her pace calm, just like Christ's wife, like God's beloved, and the power of her gaze deflected everyone's stare.[58] (3) As for Felicity, she rejoiced that she had safely given birth so that she could fight the beasts, moving from blood to blood, from midwife to gladiator,[59] about to wash in a second baptism after giving birth. (4) When they were brought to the gate and forced to wear costumes – for the men, the robes of the priests of Saturn; for the women, those of the priestesses of Ceres – that noble woman resisted

---

[57] An *agape* feast was a "love" feast; the idea for the *agape* springs from the Last Supper. An element of the meal was the subjection of the individual to the community; the meal later evolved into a meal to alleviate the needs of the poor, widows, and orphans. The context of the Carthaginian martyrs' *agape*, their last supper, powerfully evokes the Last Supper of Jesus and his apostles.

[58] Respectable Roman women were not supposed to look men straight in the eye. Perpetua's action would have been viewed as a defiant violation of societal norms. Again and again, she fails to show men the deference that they would expect to receive from a young woman. She addresses a guard "to his face," *in faciem*, for example (section 16.2; the American expression, "in someone's face," conveys the boldness of the gesture nicely). She transcends the limitations that society has imposed on her gender.

[59] The Latin here is *retiarius*, a particular type of gladiator who fought with a net, a trident, and a dagger. In the games, two gladiators (*secutores*) armed with swords and shields often competed against the *retiarius*. The *retiarius* gained the advantage over his two opponents by fighting atop a bridge-like platform called *pons*. The specific type of gladiator is worth noting since nets will soon reappear in the Passion, but to suggestively ironic effect (section 20.2). (Bomgardner suggests that it was ultimately the *retiarii* who were ordered to execute Perpetua and her friends ["Amphitheater" 90-91].)

steadfastly all the way to the end.[60] (5) She said:

"We have come here of our own will precisely so as not to have our freedom crushed; we resigned our lives precisely so as not to have to do something like this. And we made this agreement with you."

(6) Injustice recognized justice, and the tribune yielded. They were to be brought in dressed as they were before. (7) And Perpetua sang psalms, already trampling the Egyptian's head.[61] Revocatus, Saturninus, and Saturus kept threatening the gawking crowd.[62] (8) And when they came into Hilarianus' sight, by nods and gestures they began to say this:

"You condemn us, but God will condemn you."

(9) This so enraged the crowd that it demanded that a line of animal-fighters scourge them.[63] But they assuredly

---

[60] By becoming identified with cherished native deities and their cults, Saturn and Ceres managed to become (or, perhaps better, in their Punic existences, remain) two of the most important Carthaginian and African gods. This process of identification was common in the Greco-Roman world: "...local and Roman gods apparently merged with each other and were often referred to, and presumably worshipped, under a composite title...In most cases, however, we have only the record of a mixed divine name; we can only guess what that name meant, which deity (Roman or native) was uppermost in the minds of the worshippers, or whether the two had merged into a new composite whole (a process often now referred to as 'syncretism'); we do not know, in other words, how far the process was an aspect of Roman take-over (and ultimately obliteration) of native deities, how far a mutually respectful union of two divine powers, or how far it was a minimal, resistant and token incorporation of Roman imperial paraphernalia on the part of the provincials. Signs of 'syncretism,' then, always need to be interpreted. For example, to understand why most deities in the eastern part of the empire did not merge with Roman counterparts, but retained their individual personalities and characteristics, whereas in the west pre-Roman gods acquired Roman names, or non-Roman and Roman divine names were linked, we need to investigate much more deeply into the nature of Roman religion outside Rome..." (Beard, North, & Price, Religions 317-18). Rives, Roman Carthage 39-51, 132-169, provides just such a study. Most important for understanding this passage in the Passion, though, is Rives' demonstration of the importance of Ceres and Saturn to Roman Carthaginians.

[61] We are here taken back to Perpetua's athletic vision (10).

[62] Because this is Carthage and a major spectacle is being presented, we should imagine the amphitheater packed.

rejoiced in this because it meant that they had attained a share in the Lord's Passion.[64]

19. But he who said, "ask, and you shall receive,"[65] gave to those who asked the death each desired. (2) For whenever they would discuss among themselves the form of martydom they preferred, Saturninus would declare that he wished to be cast to every sort of beast, so that he could wear an even more glorious crown.[66] (3) And so, at the beginning of the spectacle, he and Revocatus endured a leopard, but they were also attacked by a bear near the platform. (4) Saturus, on the other hand, detested nothing more than the thought of a bear, and so he anticipated that a single bite of a leopard would kill him. (5) He was offered to a boar, and an animal-fighter tied him to the beast. But it was the fighter, not Saturus, who was gored. A few days after the contest, the fighter died; Saturus was merely dragged around. (6) Then he was tied up on the platform for a bear, but the bear refused to come out of its cage. And so for a second time, Saturus was called back unharmed.

---

[63] The "animal fighters," or *venatores*, were generally equipped with shields and occasionally breastplates in the second century CE, and their primary functions were to fight, hunt, or control animals during these show. How precisely they would be employed, however, depended on the requirements of a particular spectacle and on the demands of the crowd, as this passage indicates. The authorities were willing to change the course of a public show on the spot in response to the demands of the crowd, as happens more than once in the <u>Passion</u>.

[64] This evokes Jesus' scourging at the pillar: "Then Pilate took Jesus and scourged him." (John 19:1) Jesus was scourged before his crucifixion, just as the martyrs are being scourged before they face the beasts.

[65] John 16:24; cf. Matthew 7:7-10: "Ask, and it will be given you; seek, and you will find; knock, and it will be opened to you. For everyone who asks receives, and he who seeks finds, and to him who knocks it will be opened. Or what man of you, if his son asks him for bread, will give him a stone? Or if he asks for a fish, will give him a serpent?"

[66] And the Romans did, in fact, employ a considerable variety of animals in these animal shows: leopards, tigers, lions, deer, ostriches, boars, bulls, and, of course, the dreaded bears. It is left up to the reader to decide whether Saturninus' comment about wishing for greater glory should be viewed as nervous bravado, a bit of dark humor, or an oddly self-absorbed intent to please God.

20. For the young women, though, the devil had arranged a vicious heifer, an unusual but appropriate match, so that the beast's sex should rival theirs.[67] (2) They were stripped, dressed in nets, and brought out into the arena.[68] The crowd was appalled to see in this state one frail young woman and another who had just given birth and whose breasts were still dripping with milk. (3) So they were called back and dressed in unbelted robes.[69] The heifer threw Perpetua first, and she fell onto her hip. (4) Her robe had been torn on the side, and her thigh exposed. When she sat up, she covered herself, since she was more mindful of her modesty than of her pain. (5) Then she asked for a pin and fastened her disheveled hair. For it was not fitting to endure martyrdom with her hair in disarray, since she might seem to be mourning in her moment of glory.[70] (6) In this state she got up, and when she saw that Felicity had been struck down, she went to her, gave her a hand, and picked her up. And the two of them stood side by side.[71] (7) This conquered the cruelty of the crowd. So

---

[67] Clearly the authorities chose the heifer, an unusual animal for a public execution, as a cruel but pointed joke. These women, who had the temerity to step out of the familial and domestic sphere where they belonged and to flout male authority, were being reminded that they were merely women, despite their presumption. The audience would have been aware that a bull was a conventional animal employed to punish adulteresses; the authorities may have also been suggesting that Perpetua and Felicity "were not 'real women' enough to be guilty of adultery" (Shaw, "Perpetua" 7-8).

[68] Martyrdom in the Roman Empire was more awful for women than for men, since the authorities attempted to intensify the women's terror and humiliation by threatening rape and forced prostitution and through sexually charged strategies such as presenting the female martyrs stripped of their clothes. As Shaw observes, "the public denuding was a calculated move further to strip them of dignity and power." ("Perpetua" 8) There are other accounts of female martyrs enduring sexual abuse during their interrogation, sentencing, or execution. Potamiaena was threatened by her judge to be handed over to gladiators for assault (The Martyrdom of Potamiaena and Basilides 1.2 [Musurillo, Acts 132-133]). The martyr Sabrina was threatened with prostitution (The Martyrdom of Pionius and his Companions 7.8 [Musurillo, Acts 146-147]), and another, Irene, was actually brought naked to a brothel (The

the young women were called back through the Gate of Life. (8) There a man named Rusticus, who was then a catechumen and who was keeping close to Perpetua, supported her. And as if she had been asleep, she awoke, since up to that point she had been in the Spirit and in ecstasy – and she began to look around and to everyone's amazement said:

"When will we face that heifer or whatever it is?"

(9) When she heard that it had already happened, she would not be convinced until she noticed on her body and

---

Martyrdom of Agape, Irene, and Chione at Saloniki 5.8-6.3 [Musurillo, Acts 290-291]; the narrator of her martyrdom claims that no man would touch her in the brothel, thus preserving her chastity; the absence of any mention of this during her next hearing suggests otherwise).

[69] The crowd's involvement in and influence on the games is evident here. The audience was probably not horrified simply by female nudity in the arena, which was not unprecedented. Nor was it unusual for the condemned to wear nets. The text implies, rather, that it was the apparant maternity of these martyrs, with a stunning visual reminder in Felicity's case, that appalled them. For a discussion, see Salisbury, Passion 142.

[70] "The careful details and the eyewitness's interpretation of them probably reveal more about the narrator's mind than about Perpetua's. It is hard to imagine that Perpetua would have been thinking of modesty or of the appropriate hairstyle for triumphal death while being tossed by a wild beast." (Salisbury, Passion 143) Perpetua's behavior here might strike us as extremely odd (assuming that the editor has accurately reported her reactions). We will soon get evidence to suggest that she is in shock (section 20.8-9), which may help explain it. Still, modesty was extremely important to early Christian women (as it was to respectable pagan women) and should not be dismissed as a consideration in Perpetua's mind. It might be better, however, to think of her as concerned with her dignity (of which modesty was an element); Perpetua and the other martyrs were fully aware of the fact that a large audience was viewing their deaths. Martyrs naturally wanted to shake the confidence and diminish the pleasure of pagans who delighted in seeing them suffer, and they wanted to give proof of their convictions. And they were quite conscious of the fact that the way they faced death was hugely important to their fellow Christians. Preserving her dignity and the outward appearance of dignity entailed much more than the "appropriate hairstyle," and, however bizarre a twenty-first-century viewer might find Perpetua's actions, an ancient audience most likely would have admired her.

[71] Perpetua and Felicity now stand together as equals. This shows that they have cast off the status Roman society has assigned to them. Felicity, as a slave, would never have stood as Perpetua's equal, but the eyes of Christ do not recognize such distinctions.

clothes some marks from the attack.[72] (10) Then she sent for her brother and that catechumen and said to them:

"'Stand firm in your faith,'[73] love each other, and do not let our suffering weaken you."

21. Meanwhile, at another gate, Saturus was encouraging the soldier Pudens, saying:

"There is no doubt that things have turned out exactly as I had anticipated and predicted: so far, I have had nothing to do with any beasts. And so you should believe with your whole heart. Watch as I go in there and am finished off by the single bite of a leopard."

(2) Immediately, at the end of the spectacle, he was exposed to a leopard whose one bite so drenched him in blood that as he turned back the crowd screamed this testimony of his second baptism:

"Well washed! Well washed!"[74]

(3) And in fact he was well washed, who was washed in this way. (4) Then he said to the soldier Pudens:

"Farewell! Remember the faith. Remember me. Do not let these events unsettle you; rather, they should strengthen you."[75]

(5) And as Saturus spoke, he asked Pudens for the ring on his finger, dipped it into his wound, and gave it back,

---

[72] Perpetua apparently did not feel pain from the attack. It is possible that she went into shock after the initial contact. Similarly, car accident victims often cannot recall the impact. Martyrs are not infrequently depicted as experiencing a kind of anaesthesia during their ordeal (see Fox, Pagans 438). Perpetua most likely would have explained it as a consequence of the ecstasy that indicated the presence of the Holy Spirit. Whatever the explanation for this phenomenon, it was not uncommon among martyrs.

[73] 1 Cor 16:13; the entire passage: "Be watchful, stand firm in your faith, be courageous, be strong. Let all that you do be done in love." (16:13-14)

[74] Apparently a greeting of good omen after a bath, as an inscription from Brescia in Italy testifies (Dessau, Inscriptiones Latinae Selectae 5725; cited in Musurillo. p. 131, no. 21). The crowd, of course, is being cruelly ironic.

[75] This is a reference to both 1 Corinthians 16:13 and Acts 14:22: "strengthening the souls of the disciples, exhorting them to continue in the faith, and saying that through many tribulations we must enter the kingdom of God."

leaving this inheritance behind as a pledge and reminder of his blood.[76] (6) Then he was tossed on the ground in the usual place with the others to have their throats cut.[77] (7) But the crowd demanded that they be brought back out into the arena, so that their eyes might be accomplices to the sword as it penetrated the martyrs' flesh. And so the martyrs got up of their own accord, went to the spot the crowd had indicated, and kissed each other, so that they could complete their martyrdom with the ritual kiss of peace. (8) The others received the sword unmoving and in silence, particularly Saturus, who was the first to ascend and release his soul. Yet again he waited for Perpetua. (9) She, however, in order that she taste some pain, screamed when the sword pierced her to the bone. Then she herself guided the trembling right hand of the inexperienced gladiator to her own throat. (10) Perhaps so great a woman, who was feared by the unclean spirit, could not have been killed, unless she herself had wished it. (11) O most brave and blessed martyrs! O truly called and chosen for the glory of our Lord Jesus Christ! Anyone who exalts and honors and adores this glory should most certainly read these examples, examples undoubtedly of no less importance for the edification of the Church than those of old. For these recent events will also affirm that the one and always the same Holy Spirit still works even now, and God the Father and his son, Jesus Christ our Lord, whose splendor and immense power are forever and ever. Amen.

---

[76] Saturus dips Pudens' ring in his own blood in order to give Pudens a tangible reminder of his suffering as a martyr. This offering of his own blood could be seen as mirroring Christ's offering of his blood at the Last Supper, when he says, "This is my blood of the covenant, which is poured out for many." (Mark 14:24)

[77] The "usual place" for killing the condemned was called the *spoliarium*, beyond the *Porta Libitinensis* described earlier (see footnote at section 10.13). Those who survived the onslaught of attacks in the arena were taken to the *spoliarium* to be slain. The dead were also taken to this place and subsequently buried. In this passage, the crowd again asserts its power by forcing a public execution of the Christians (Bomgardner, "Amphitheater" 89).

A Word on the
Translation and Notes

■

    This translation attempts to address three different, and at times conflicting, priorities. We aim to (1) convey accurately the precise meaning of the original Latin, (2) express its general sense, feeling, and import, and (3) render the text's Latin into contemporary American English that is accessible and engaging. When these priorities have clashed, we have elected not to render the Latin literally but to provide a version that preserves what we believe the authors were trying to convey. Translation is always interpretation. We hope that the martyrs, and in particular Perpetua and Saturus who actually wrote much of this Passion, will forgive these liberties. Modern readers of this translation can remedy its shortcomings by reading the remarkable original Latin text, which is included at the end of this book. Ideally, the prospect of meeting Perpetua and her friends in their own words will motivate those who have not yet studied Latin to learn the language.

    The translation and notes are the result of an advanced Latin seminar at Loyola College in Maryland, "Resistance to Rome: Perpetua's Passion." They are the work of the students in the seminar. We translated the entire work without the aid of earlier translations but found that ours in some places closely parallels already existing translations. Where that has turned out to be the case, we have nonetheless retained our translation, since it seemed to us counterproductive and artificial to change our translation's language just to distinguish it from others. In some cases, we believe, the similarities among translations are attributable to the clarity and straightforwardness of the Latin, particularly Perpetua's.

<u>Perpetua's Passion</u> has three authors: Perpetua herself, her fellow martyr Saturus, and an editor. The Latin of the three can be quite different. The greatest contrast is between Perpetua's exquisitely direct prose and the editor's highly rhetorical, at times somewhat convoluted style. For the most part, we did not seek to clarify through translation the editor's occasionally obscure Latin and thought.

For quotations from the Bible, this text employs the Revised Standard Version translation.

The notes and introduction to this text are intended for non-specialists and assume that many readers will be unfamiliar with the history of the Roman Empire, Carthage, early Christianity, and the vexed relations between the Christians and their pagan neighbors. Given the scope of this volume, however, most issues will be addressed only briefly. Readers will find in the "Recommended Reading" a list of books and articles that supplement the information we provide and offer other approaches to and interpretations of the text.

A Word on the Text

For the most part, we have used the Latin text of <u>Perpetua's Passion</u> from C. J. M. J. van Beek's <u>Passio Sanctarum Perpetuae et Felicitatis</u> (Dekker & Van de Vegt S. A., 1936), which also provides the most useful discussion of the history of the manuscripts and earlier editions (pp. 17*-148*). A Greek version of Perpetua's martyrdom has also survived, and some have taken it to be the original. Most scholars and readers are convinced that the Latin text is the original, and we agree. We have, thus, used the Latin for our translation, although we have consulted the Greek here and there for clarification. For an early English-language argument that the Greek is the original, see J. Rendel Harris & Seth K. Gifford, <u>The Acts of the Martyrdom of Perpetua and Felicitas: The Original Greek Text</u> (C. J. Clay and Sons, 1890) 13-18; Harris discovered the manuscript in Jerusalem (Robinson, <u>Passion</u> 3, note 1, however, asserts that Harris has authorized him to say that Harris "has seen reason to change his view of the matter, and to regard the Latin as the original"; Robinson also presents arguments supporting the priority of the Latin version [2-9]). The most important defense of this position is by Louis Robert, "Une vision de Perpétue, martyre a Carthage en 203,"

Comptes rendus de L'Académie des Inscriptions et Belles-Lettres (1982) 228-278.

The Latin and Greek texts can easily be compared since Van Beek has set them side-by-side on facing pages (4-53). He also provides the two texts of the Acta SS. Perpetuae et Felicitatis [58-73], an indisputably later condensation and rewriting of Perpetua's Passion. The Acta SS. Perpetuae et Felicitatis tells us more about later Christians' attempts to make sense of and even "correct" Perpetua than it does about Perpetua and her friends (see Shaw, "Perpetua" 33-36).

Recommended Reading

The bibliography on Perpetua's trials, the persecution of the early Christians, their practice and beliefs, the Roman province of Africa and the city of Carthage, the status and lives of Roman women – all topics essential to making sense of Perpetua's death – is immense. The scope and purpose of this volume, unfortunately, do not permit the inclusion of a complete bibliography of all the works that have contributed to our understanding of these topics and might help readers eager to explore more thoroughly the events of 203 CE and their meaning. Included below, then, are some of the most important, useful, and accessible works, those that will be particularly valuable to readers new to the topic, and those that have been particularly valuable to us in preparing this book.

Readers who pursue this topic further will find that opinions differ widely on the nature, extent, and causes of the persecutions of the early Christians. This is not surprising, since our sources are very few and fragmentary, and their views of the situation tend to be limited and partisan. Modern historians are sometimes compelled to fill in huge blanks and too often to appeal to what seems reasonable rather than what the evidence indicates. In our age, moreover, religious passions run hot, and so scholars' and other writers' religious convictions or lack thereof have a considerable affect on how they see the early Christians; passion and conviction also, at times, make the debates contentious.

general reference

The Encyclopedia of Early Christianity 2nd edition (Everett Ferguson, ed.; Garland, 1997)

The New Catholic Encyclopedia 2nd edition (Thomson/Gale, 2003)

Beard, Mary, North, John, & Price, Simon, Religions of Rome 2 volumes (Cambridge University Press, 1998)

Chirat, Henri, Dictionnaire Latin-Français des Auteurs Chrétiens (Brepols, 1954)

on Perpetua's Passion

Dölger, F. J., "Antike Parallelen zum leidenden Dinocrates in der Passio Perpetuae," Antike und Christentum 2 (1930) 1-40

-----, "Der Kampf mit dem Ägypter in der Perpetua-Vision: das Martyrium als Kampf mit dem Teufel," Antike und Christentum 3 (1932) 177-88

Frend, W. H. C., "Blandina and Perpetua: Two Early Christian Heroines," in Women in Early Christianity (ed., D. M. Scholer; Garland, 1993)

Harris, J. Rendel & Gifford, Seth K., The Acts of the Martyrdom of Perpetua and Felicitas: The Original Greek Text (C. J. Clay and Sons, 1890)

Robert, Louis, "Une vision de Perpétue, martyre à Carthage en 203," Comptes rendus de L'Académie des Inscriptions et Belles-Lettres (1982) 228-278

Robinson, J. Armitage, <u>The Passion of Perpetua</u>
(Cambridge University Press, 1891)

Salisbury, Joyce E., <u>Perpetua's Passion. The Death and
Memory of a Young Roman Woman</u> Routledge,
1997)

Shaw, Brent D., "The Passion of Perpetua," <u>Past and
Present</u> 139 (1993) 3-45

on martyrdom and martyr acts

Barnes, Timothy, "Pre-Decian <u>Acta Martyrum</u>,"
reprinted in Barnes, <u>Early Christianity and
The Roman Empire</u> (Ashgate Variorum, 1984; essay
originally published in 1968) essay I

Fox, Robin Lane, <u>Pagans and Christians</u> (Knopf, 1987)

Musurillo, Herbert, <u>Acts of the Christian Martyrs</u>
(Oxford University Press, 1972)

Shaw, Brent, "Body/Power/Identity: Passions of the
Martyrs," <u>Journal of Early Christian Studies</u> 4
(Fall, 1996) 269-312

Tabbernee, William, "Early Montanism and Voluntary
Martyrdom," <u>The Australian and New Zealand
Theological Review</u> 19 (1985) 33-44

Wansink, Craig S. <u>Chained in Christ. The Experience
and Rhetoric of Paul's Imprisonments</u> (<u>Journal
for the Study of the New Testament</u>; Supplement
Series 130; Sheffield Academic Press, 1996)

on the religious life of Roman Carthage

Barnes, Timothy, <u>Tertullian. A Historical and Literary
Study</u> (Oxford University Press, 1985; revised edition with "Tertullian Revisited: A Postscript")

Rives, James, <u>Religion and Authority in Roman
Carthage from Augustus to Constantine</u> (Oxford

University Press, 1995)

Toutain, J. Les cultes païens dans l'empire romain (3
volumes; Paris, 1907-1920)

on Roman Africa and Carthage

Raven, Susan, Rome in Africa (Routledge, 1993)

Warmington, B. H., Carthage: A History (Barnes &
Noble, 1993)

on contests and spectacles

Auguet, Roland, Cruelty and Civilization: The Roman
Games (Routledge, 1994)

Bomgardner, David L., "The Carthage Amphitheater:
A Reappraisal," American Journal of Archaeology
93 (1989) 85-103

Golvin, Jean-Claude, L'Amphithéâtre Romain
(Boccard, 1988)

Kyle, Donald G., Spectacles of Death in Ancient
Rome (Routledge, 1998)

Veyne, Paul, Bread and Circuses (trans. B. Pearce;
Penguin, 1990)

Wiedemann, Thomas, Emperors and Gladiators
(Routledge, 1992)

on the Roman authorities

Birley, Anthony, Septimius Severus. The African
Emperor (Eyre & Spottiswoode, 1971)

Rives, James, "The Piety of a Persecutor," Journal of
Early Christian Studies 4.1 (1996) 1-26

on persecution

Barnes, Timothy, "Legislation against the Christians,"
reprinted in Barnes, Early Christianity and

The Roman Empire (Ashgate Variorum, 1984; essay
  originally published in 1968) essay II
de Ste. Croix, G. E. M., "Why Were the Early
  Christians Persecuted?" Past and Present 26
  (1963) 6-38
-----, "A Rejoinder" Past and Present 27 (1964) 28-33
Frend, W. H. C., Martyrdom and Persecution in the
  Early Church (Basil Blackwell, 1965)
-----, "A Severan Persecution? Evidence of the Historia
  Augusta," in Forma Futuri: Studi in Onore del
  Cardinale Michele Pellegrino (1975) 470-489
Sherwin-White, A. N, "An Amendment," Past and
  Present 27 (1964) 23-27

on pagan views of early Christianity
Labriolle, Pierre de, La réaction païenne, étude sur la
  polémique antichrétienne du Ier au VI siècle
  (2nd ed.; Paris, 1948)
Walsh, Joseph, "On Christian Atheism," Vigiliae
  Christianae 45 (1991) 255-277
Walsh, Joseph, & Gottlieb, Gunther, "Zur
  Christenfrage im zweiten Jahrhundert," in
  Gunther Gottlieb & Pedro Barceló, Christen und
  Heiden in Staat und Gesellschaft des zweiten bis
  vierten Jahrhunderts (Ernst Vögel, 1992) 3-86
Wilken, Robert L., The Christians as the Romans
  Saw Them (New Haven/London; Yale University
  Press, 1984)

on ancient women
Hallett, Judith, Fathers and Daughters in Roman
  Society (Princeton University Press, 1984)

Lefkowitz, Mary R., & Fant, M. B., <u>Women's Lives in Greece and Rome</u> (Johns Hopkins University Press, 1982)

Pomeroy, Sarah B., <u>Goddesses, Whores, Wives and Slaves: Women in Classical Antiquity</u> (Schocken, 1975)

on ancient Christian women

Aspegren, Kerstin, <u>The Male Woman. A Feminine Ideal in the Early Church</u> (Acta Universitatis Upsaliensis; Almqvist & Wiksell International, 1990)

Bassler, Jouette, "The Widow's Tale: A Fresh Look at 1 Tim 5:3-16," <u>Journal of Biblical Literature</u> 103.1 (1984) 23-41

Dronke, Peter, <u>Women Writers of the Middle Ages</u> (Cambridge University Press, 1984)

Fiorenza, Elizabeth Schüssler, "'You are not to be called Father.' Early Christian History in a Feminist Perspective," <u>Cross Currents</u> 29.3 (1979) 301-23

----, <u>In Memory of Her. A Feminist Theological Reconstruction of Christian Origins</u> (Crossroad, 1983/1992)

Hall, Stuart G., "Women among the Martyrs," in <u>Christianity in Relation to Jews, Greeks, and Romans</u> (ed. Everett Ferguson; Garland, 1999) 301-321

Klawiter, Frederick C., "The Role of Martyrdom and Persecution in Developing the Priestly Authority of Women in Early Christianity," <u>Church History</u> 49.3 (September, 1980) 251-261

Kraemer, Ross, <u>Her share of the Blessings</u> (Oxford University Press, 1992)

Wilken, Robert, <u>The Spirit of Christian Thought. Seeking the Face of God</u> (Yale University Press, 2003)

other

Dickie, Matthew, <u>Magic and Magicians in the Greco-Roman World</u> (Routledge, 2001)

Fowl, Stephen, "Paul's Reposte to Fr. Rodrigues: Conceptions of Martyrdom in Philippians and Endo's <u>Silence</u>," in <u>Postmodern Interpretations of the Bible</u> (ed. A. K. M. Adam; Chalice Press, 2001) 243-53

Sherwin White, A. N. <u>Roman Society and Roman Law in the New Testament</u> (Oxford University Press, 1963)

White, Robert J. <u>The Interpretation of Dreams: Oneirocritica by Artemidorus</u> (Noyes Classical Studies; Noyes Press, 1975)

Appendix I: The Latin Text

■

1. Si uetera fidei exempla et Dei gratiam testificantia et aedificationem hominis operantia propterea in litteris sunt digesta ut lectione eorum quasi repraesentatione rerum et Deus honoretur et homo confortetur, cur non et noua documenta aeque utrique causae conuenientia et digerantur? **2.** Uel quia proinde et haec uetera futura quandoque sunt et necessaria posteris, si in praesenti suo tempore minori deputantur auctoritati propter praesumptam uenerationem antiquitatis. **3.** Sed uiderint qui unam uirtutem Spiritus unius Sancti pro aetatibus iudicent temporum, cum maiora reputanda sunt nouitiora quaeque ut nouissimiora secundum exuperationem gratiae in ultima saeculi spatia decretam. **4.** In nouissimis enim diebus, dicit dominus, effundam de Spiritu meo super omnem carnem, et prophetabunt filii filiaeque eorum; et super seruos et ancillas meas de meo Spiritu effundam; et iuuenes uisiones uidebunt, et senes somnia somniabunt. **5.** Itaque et nos qui sicut prophetias ita et uisiones nouas pariter repromissas et agnoscimus et honoramus ceterasque uirtutes Spiritus Sancti ad instrumentum Ecclesiae deputamus (cui et missus est idem omnia donatiua administraturus in omnibus, prout unicuique dis-

tribuit dominus) necessario et digerimus et ad gloriam Dei
lectione celebramus, ut ne qua aut inbecillitas aut desperatio
fidei apud ueteres tantum aestimet gratiam diuinitatis conu-
ersatam, sive in martyrum siue in reuelationum dignatione,
cum semper Deus operetur quae repromisit, non credentibus in testimonium, credentibus in beneficium. 6. Et nos
itaque quod audiuimus et contretauimus, annuntiamus et
uobis, fratres et filioli, uti et uos qui interfuistis rememor-
emini gloriae domini et qui nunc cognoscitis per auditum
communionem habeatis cum sanctis martyribus, et per illos
cum domino nostro Iesu Christo, cui est claritas et honor
in saecula saeculorum. Amen.

2. Apprehensi sunt adolescentes catechumeni, Reuocatus
et Felicitas, conserua eius, Saturninus et Secundulus. Inter
hos et Vibia Perpetua, honeste nata, liberaliter instituta,
matronaliter nupta, (2.) habens patrem et matrem et fratres
duos, alterum aeque catechumenum, et filium infantem
ad ubera. 3. Erat autem ipsa circiter annorum uiginti duo.
Haec ordinem totum martyrii sui iam hinc ipsa narrauit
sicut conscriptum manu sua et suo sensu reliquit.

3. Cum adhuc, inquit, cum prosecutoribus essemus et
me pater uerbis euertere cupiret et deicere pro sua affectione
perseueraret:
Pater, inquam, uides uerbi gratia uas hoc iacens, urceo-
lum siue aliud?
Et dixit:
Video.
2. Et ego dixi ei:
Numquid alio nomine uocari potest quam quod est?
et ait:
Non.

Sic et ego aliud me dicere non possum nisi quod sum, Christiana.

3. Tunc pater motus hoc uerbo mittit se in me ut oculos mihi erueret, sed uexauit tantum est profectus et uictus cum argumentis diaboli. 4. Tunc paucis diebus quod caruissem patre, domino gratias egi et refrigeraui absentia illius. 5. In ipso spatio paucorum dierum baptizati sumus, et mihi Spiritus dictauit non aliud petendum ab aqua nisi sufferentiam carnis. Post paucos dies recipimur in carcerem; et expaui, quia numquam experta eram tales tenebras. 6. O diem asperum: aestus ualidus turbarum beneficio, concussurae militum. Nouissime macerabar sollicitudine infantis ibi. 7. Tunc Tertius et Pomponius, benedicti diaconi qui nobis ministrabant, constituerunt praemio uti paucis horis emissi in meliorem locum carceris refrigeraremus. 8. Tunc exeuntes de carcere uniuersi sibi uacabant. Ego infantem lactabam iam inedia defectum; sollicita pro eo adloquebar matrem et confortabam fratrem, commendabam filium; tabescebam ideo quod illos tabescere uideram mei beneficio. 9. Tales sollicitudines multis diebus passa sum; et usurpaui ut mecum infans in carcere maneret; et statim conualui et releuata sum a labore et sollicitudine infantis, et factus est mihi carcer subito praetorium, ut ibi mallem esse quam alicubi.

4. Tunc dixit mihi frater meus:

Domina soror, iam in magna dignatione es, tanta ut postules uisionem et ostendatur tibi an passio sit an commeatus.

2. Et ego quae me sciebam fabulari cum Domino, cuius beneficia tanta experta eram, fidenter repromisi ei dicens:

Crastina die tibi renuntiabo.

Et postulaui, et ostensum est mihi hoc. 3. Uideo scalam

aeream mirae magnitudinis pertingentem usque ad caelum et angustam, per quam nonnisi singuli ascendere possent, et in lateribus scalae omne genus ferramentorum infixum. Erant ibi gladii, Lanceae, hami, machaerae, ueruta, ut si quis neglegenter aut non sursum adtendens ascenderet, laniaretur et carnes eius in haererent ferramentis. 4. Et erat sub ipsa scala draco cubans mirae magnitudinis, qui ascendentibus insidias praestabat et exterrebat ne ascenderent. 5. Ascendit autem Saturus prior, qui postea se propter nos ultro tradiderat (quia ipse nos aedificauerat), et tunc cum adducti sumus, praesens non fuerat. 6. Et peruenit in caput scalae et conuertit se et dixit mihi:

Perpetua, sustineo te; sed uide ne te mordeat draco ille.

Et dixi ego:

Non me nocebit in nomine Iesu Christi.

7. Et desub ipsa scala, quasi timens me, lente eiecit caput. Et quasi primum gradum calcarem, calcaui illi caput et ascendi. 8. Et uidi spatium immensum horti et in medio sedentem hominem canum in habitu pastoris, grandem, oues mulgentem. Et circumstantes candidati milia multa. 9. Et leuauit caput et aspexit me et dixit mihi:

Bene venisti, τέκνον.

Et clamauit me et de caseo quod mulgebat dedit mihi quasi buccellam; et ego accepi iunctis manibus et manducaui; et uniuersi circumstantes dixerunt:

Amen.

10. Et ad sonum uocis experrecta sum, conmanducans adhuc dulce nescio quid. Et retuli statim fratri meo; et intelleximus passionem esse futuram, et coepimus nullam iam spem in saeculo habere.

5. Post paucos dies rumor cucurrit ut audiremur.

Superuenit autem et de ciuitate pater meus, consumptus taedio, et ascendit ad me, ut me deiceret, dicens:

(2.) Miserere, filia, canis meis; Miserere patri, si dignus sum a te pater uocari; si his te manibus ad hunc florem aetatis prouexi, si te praeposui omnibus fratribus tuis: ne me dederis in dedecus hominum. 3. Aspice fratres tuos, aspice matrem tuam et materteram, aspice filium tuum qui post te uiuere non poterit. 4. Depone animos; ne uniuersos nos extermines. Nemo enim nostrum libere loquetur, si tu aliquid fueris passa.

5. Haec dicebat quasi pater pro sua pietate basians mihi manus et se ad pedes meos iactans et lacrimans me iam non filiam nominabat sed dominam. 6. Et ego dolebam casum patris mei quod solus de passione mea gauisurus non esset de toto genere meo. Et confortaui eum dicens:

Hoc fiet in illa catasta quod Deus uoluerit. Scito enim nos non in nostra esse potestate constitutos, sed in Dei.

Et recessit a me contristatus.

6. Alio die cum pranderemus, subito rapti sumus ut audiremur. Et peruenimus ad forum. Rumor statim per uicinas fori partes cucurrit et factus est populus inmensus. 2. Ascendimus in catastam. Interrogati ceteri confessi sunt. Uentum est et ad me. Et apparuit pater ilico cum filio meo et extraxit me de gradu dicens:

Supplica. Miserere infanti.

3. Et Hilarianus procurator, qui tunc loco proconsulis Minuci Timiniani defuncti ius gladii acceperat,

Parce, inquit, canis patris tui, parce infantiae pueri. Fac sacrum pro salute imperatorum.

4. Et ego respondi:

Non facio.

Hilarianus:

Christiana es?

Inquit. Et ego respondi:

Christiana sum.

5. Et cum staret pater ad me deiciendam, iussus est ab Hilariano proici et uirga percussus est. et doluit mihi casus patris mei quasi ego fuissem percussa; sic dolui pro senecta eius misera. 6. Tunc nos uniuersos pronuntiat et damnat ad bestias; et hilares descendimus ad carcerem. 7. Tunc quia consueuerat a me infans mammas accipere et mecum in carcere manere, statim mitto ad patrem Pomponium diaconum, postulans infantem. Sed pater dare noluit. 8. Et quomodo Deus uoluit, neque ille amplius mammas desiderauit neque mihi feruorem fecerunt ne sollicitudine infantis et dolore mammarum macerarer.

7. Post dies paucos, dum uniuersi oramus, subito media oratione profecta est mihi uox et nominaui Dinocraten.

Et obstipui quod numquam mihi in mentem uenisset nisi tunc, et dolui commemorata casus eius. 2. Et cognoui me statim dignam esse et pro eo petere debere. Et coepi de ipso orationem facere multum et ingemescere ad dominum. 3. Continuo ipsa nocte ostensum est mihi hoc. 4. Uideo Dinocraten exeuntem de loco tenebroso ubi et conplures erant, aestuantem ualde et sitientem, sordido cultu et colore pallido; et uulnus in facie eius, quod cum moreretur habuit. 5. Hic Dinocrates fuerat frater meus carnalis, annorum septem, qui per infirmitatem facie cancerata male obiit ita ut mors eius odio fuerit omnibus hominibus. 6. Pro hoc ergo orationem feceram; et inter me et illum grande erat diastema ita ut uterque ad inuicem accedere non possemus. 7. Erat deinde in illo loco ubi Dinocrates erat piscina plena aqua, altiorem marginem habens quam erat statura pueri; et extendebat se Dinocrates quasi bibiturus. 8. Ego dolebam

quod et piscina illa aquam habebat et tamen propter altitu-
dinem marginis bibiturus non esset. 9. Et experrecta sum, et
cognoui fratrem meum laborare. Sed fidebam me profutur-
am labori eius. Et orabam pro eo omnibus diebus quousque
transiuimus in carcerem castrensem. Munere enim castrensi
eramus pugnaturi; natale tunc Getae Caesaris. 10. Et feci
pro illo orationem die et nocte gemens et lacrimans ut mihi
donaretur.

8. Die quo in neruo mansimus, ostensum est mihi
hoc. Uideo locum illum quem retro uideram et Dinocraten
mundo corpore bene uestitum refrigerantem; et ubi erat
uulnus uideo cicatricem, (2.) et piscinam illam, quam retro
uideram, summisso margine usque ad umbilicum pueri; et
aquam de ea trahebat sine cessatione. 3. Et super marginem
fiala aurea plena aqua. Et accessit Dinocrates et de ea bibere
coepit; quae fiala non deficiebat. 4. Et satiatus accessit de
aqua ludere more infantium gaudens. Et experrecta sum.
Tunc intellexi translatum eum esse de poena.

9. Deinde post dies paucos Pudens miles optio, prae-
positus carceris, nos magnificare coepit intellegens magnam
uirtutem esse in nobis; qui multos ad nos admittebat ut et
nos et illi inuicem refrigeraremus. 2. Ut autem proximauit
dies muneris, intrat ad me pater meus consumptus taedio,
et coepit barbam suam euellere et in terram mittere, et
prosternere se in faciem, et inproperare annis suis, et dicere
tanta uerba quae mouerent uniuersam creaturam. 3. Ego
dolebam pro infelici senecta eius.

10. Pridie quam pugnaremus, uideo in horomate hoc:
venisse Pomponium diaconum ad ostium carceris et pulsare
uehementer. 2. Et exiui ad eum et aperui ei; qui erat uestitus

discincta candida, habens multiplices galliculas. 3. et dixit mihi:

Perpetua, te expectamus; ueni.

Et tenuit mihi manum et coepimus ire per aspera loca et flexuosa. 4. Uix tandem peruenimus anhelantes ad amphitheatrum et induxit me in media arena et dixit mihi:

Noli pauere. Hic sum tecum et conlaboro tecum.

Et abiit. 5. Et aspicio populum ingentem adtonitum; et quia sciebam me ad bestias damnatam esse, mirabar quod non mitterentur mihi bestiae. 6. Et exiuit quidam contra me Aegyptius foedus specie cum adiutoribus suis pugnaturus mecum. Ueniunt et ad me adolescentes decori, adiutores et fautores mei. 7. Et expoliata sum et facta sum masculus; et coeperunt me fauisores mei oleo defricare, quomodo solent in agone. Et illum contra Aegyptium uideo in afa uolutantem. 8. Et exiuit uir quidam mirae magnitudinis ut etiam excederet fastigium amphitheatri, discinctatus, purpuram inter duos clauos per medium pectus habens, et galliculas multiformes ex auro et argento factas, et ferens uirgam quasi lanista, et ramum uiridem in quo erant mala aurea. 9. Et petiit silentium et dixit:

Hic Aegyptius, si hanc uicerit, occidet illam gladio; haec, si hunc uicerit, accipiet ramum istum. 10. Et recessit. Et accessimus ad inuicem et coepimus mittere pugnos. Ille mihi pedes adprehendere uolebat; ego autem illi calcibus faciem caedebam. 11. Et sublata sum in aere et coepi eum sic caedere quasi terram non calcans. At ubi uidi moram fieri, iunxi manus ut digitos in digitos mitterem et apprehendi illi caput; et cecidit in faciem et calcaui illi caput. 12. Et coepit populus clamare et fauisores mei psallere. Et accessi ad lanistam et accepi ramum. 13. Et osculatus est me et dixit mihi: Filia, pax tecum.

Et coepi ire cum gloria ad portam Sanauiuariam. Et

experrecta sum. 14. Et intellexi me non ad bestias, sed contra diabolum esse pugnaturam; sed sciebam mihi esse uictoriam. 15. Hoc usque in pridie muneris egi; ipsius autem muneris actum, si quis uoluerit, scribat.

11. Sed et Saturus benedictus hanc uisionem suam edidit, quam ipse conscripsit. 2. Passi, inquit, eramus, et exiuimus de carne, et coepimus ferri a quattuor angelis in orientem, quorum manus nos non tangebant. 3. Ibamus autem non supini sursum uersi, sed quasi mollem cliuum ascendentes. 4. Et liberato primo mundo uidimus lucem inmensam, et dixi Perpetuae (erat enim haec in latere meo):

Hoc est quod nobis Dominus promittebat: percepimus promissionem.

5. Et dum gestamur ab ipsis quattuor angelis, factum est nobis spatium grande, quod tale fuit quasi uiridiarium arbores habens rosae et omne genus flores. 6. Altitudo arborum erat in modum cypressi, quarum folia cadebant sine cessatione. 7. Ibi autem in uiridiario alii quattuor angeli fuerunt clariores ceteris: qui, ubi uiderunt nos, honorem nobis dederunt, et dixerunt ceteris angelis,

Ecce sunt, ecce sunt, cum admiratione.

Et expauescentes quattuor illi angeli qui gestabant nos, deposuerunt nos. 8. Et pedibus nostris transiuimus ad stadium uia lata. 9. Ibi inuenimus Iocundum et Saturninum et Artaxium, qui eadem persecutione uiui arserunt, et Quintum, qui et ipse martyr in carcere exierat. Et quaerebamus de illis, ubi essent. 10. Ceteri angeli dixerunt nobis:

Venite prius, introite, et salutate Dominum.

12. Et uenimus prope locum cuius loci parietes tales erant quasi de luce aedificati; et ante ostium loci illius angeli quattuor stabant, qui introeuntes uestierunt stolas candidas. 2. Et introiuimus, et audiuimus uocem unitam dicentem,

ἅγιος, ἅγιος, ἅγιος

sine cessatione. 3. Et uidimus in eodem loco sedentem quasi hominem canum, niueos habentem capillos et uultu iuuenili, cuius pedes non uidimus. 4. Et in dextera et in sinistra seniores quattuor, et post illos ceteri seniores complures stabant. 5. Et introeuntes cum admiratione stetimus ante thronum, et quattuor angeli subleuauerunt nos et osculati sumus illum, et de manu sua traiecit nobis in faciem. 6. Et ceteri seniores dixerunt nobis:

Stemus.

et stetimus et pacem fecimus. et dixerunt nobis seniores:

Ite e ludite.

7. Et dixi Perpetuae:

Habes quod uis.

Et dixit mihi:

Deo gratias, ut quomodo in carne hilaris fui, hilarior sim et hic modo.

13. Et exiuimus et uidimus ante fores Optatum episcopum ad dexteram et Aspasium presbyterum doctorem ad sinistram separatos et tristes. 2. et miserunt se ad pedes nobis et dixerunt:

Componite inter nos, quia existis, et sic nos reliquistis.

3. Et diximus illis:

Non tu es papa noster et tu presbyter, ut uos ad pedes nobis mittatis?

Et moti sumus et complexi illos sumus. 4. Et coepit Perpetua graece cum illis loqui, et segregauimus eos in uiridiarium sub arbore rosae. 5. Et dum loquimur cum eis, dixerunt illis angeli:

Sinite illos refrigerent; et si quas habetis inter uos dissensiones, dimittite uobis inuicem.

6. Et conturbauerunt eos. Et dixerunt Optato:

Corrige plebem tuam, quia sic ad te conueniunt quasi de circo redeuntes et de factionibus certantes.

7. Et sic nobis uisum est quasi uellent claudere portas. 8. Et coepimus illic multos fratres cognoscere sed et martyras. Uniuersi odore inenarrabili alebamur qui nos satiabat. Tunc gaudens experrectus sum.

14. Hae uisiones insigniores ipsorum martyrum beatissimorum Saturi et Perpetuae, quas ipsi conscripserunt. 2. Secundulum uero Deus maturiore exitu de saeculo adhuc in carcere euocauit non sine gratia ut bestias lucraretur. 3. Gladium tamen etsi non anima certe caro eius agnouit.

15. Circa Felicitatem uero et illi gratia domini eiusmodi contigit. 2. cum octo iam mensium uentrem haberet (nam praegnans fuerat adprehensa), instante spectaculi die in magno erat luctu ne propter uentrem differretur (quia non licet praegnantes poenae repraesentari) et ne inter alios postea sceleratos sanctum et innocentem sanguinem funderet. 3. Sed et conmartyres grauiter contristabantur ne tam bonam sociam quasi comitem solam in uia eiusdem spei relinquerent. 4. Coniuncto itaque unito gemitu ad Dominum orationem fuderunt ante tertium diem muneris. 5. Statim post orationem dolores inuaserunt. Et cum pro naturali difficultate octaui mensis in partu laborans doleret, ait illi quidam ex ministris cataractariorum:

Quae sic modo doles, quid facies obiecta bestiis, quas contempsisti cum sacrificare noluisti?

6. Et illa respondit:

Modo ego patior quod patior; illic autem alius erit in me qui patietur pro me, quia et ego pro illo passura sum.

7. Ita enixa est puellam, quam sibi quaedam soror in filiam educauit.

16. Quoniam ergo permisit et permittendo uoluit Spiritus Sanctus ordinem ipsius muneris conscribi, etsi indigni ad supplementum tantae gloriae describendae, tamen quasi mandatum sanctissimae Perpetuae, immo fideicommissum eius exequimur, unum adicientes documentum de ipsius constantia et animi sublimitate. 2. Cum tribunus castigatius eos castigaret, quia ex admonitionibus hominum uanissimorum uerebatur ne subtraherentur de carcere incantationibus aliquibus magicis, in faciem ei Perpetua respondit:

(3.) Quid utique non permittis nobis refrigerare noxiis nobilissimis, Caesaris scilicet, et natali eiusdem pugnaturis? Aut non tua Gloria est, si pinguiores illo producamur?

4. Horruit et erubuit tribunus; et ita iussit illos humanius haberi ut fratribus eius et ceteris facultas fieret introeundi et refrigerandi cum eis, iam et ipso optione carceris credente.

17. Pridie quoque cum illam cenam ultimam quam liberam uocant, quantum in ipsis erat, non cenam liberam sed agapem cenarent, eadem constantia ad populum uerba iactabant, comminantes iudicium Dei, contestantes passionis suae felicitatem, inridentes concurrentium curiositatem, dicente Saturo:

(2.) Crastinus satis uobis non est? quid libenter uidetis quod odistis? Hodie amici, cras inimici. Notate tamen uobis facies nostras diligenter, ut recognoscatis nos in die illo.

3. Ita omnes inde adtoniti discedebant, ex quibus multi crediderunt.

18. Illuxit dies uictoriae illorum, et processerunt de carcere in amphitheatrum quasi in caelum hilares, uultu decori, si forte gaudio pauentes non timore. 2. Sequebatur Perpetua lucido *uultu* et placido incessu ut matrona Christi, ut Dei delicata, uigore oculorum deiciens omnium conspectum. 3. Item Felicitas, saluam se peperisse gaudens ut ad bestias pugnaret, a sanguine ad sanguinem, ab obstetrice ad retiarium, lotura post partum baptismo secundo. 4. Et cum ducti essent in portam et cogerentur habitum induere, uiri quidem sacerdotum Saturni, feminae uero sacratarum Cereri, generosa illa in finem usque constantia repugnauit. 5. Dicebat enim:

Ideo ad hoc sponte peruenimus ne libertas nostra obduceretur; ideo animam nostram addiximus, ne tale aliquid faceremus; hoc uobiscum pacti sumus.

6. Agnouit iniustitia iustitiam: concessit tribunus. Quomodo erant, simpliciter inducerentur. 7. Perpetua psallebat caput iam Aegyptii calcans. Reuocatus et Saturnius et Saturus populo spectanti comminabantur. 8. Dehinc ut sub conspectu Hilariani peruenerunt, gestu et nutu coeperunt Hilariano dicere:

Tu nos, inquiunt, te autem Deus.

9. Ad hoc populus exasperatus flagellis eos uexari per ordinem uenatorum postulauit; et utique gratulati sunt quod aliquid et de dominicis passionibus essent consecuti.

19. Sed qui dixerat: Petite et accipietis, petentibus dederat eum exitum quem quis desiderauerat. 2. Nam, si quando inter se de martyrii sui uoto sermocinabantur, Saturninus quidem omnibus bestiis uelle se obici profitebatur, ut scilicet gloriosiorem gestaret coronam. 3. Itaque in commissione spectaculi ipse et Reuocatus leopardum experti etiam super pulpitum ab urso uexati sunt. 4. Saturus autem nihil magis quam ursum

abominabatur; sed uno morsu leopardi confici se iam prae-
sumebat. 5. Itaque cum apro subministraretur, uenator potius
qui illum apro subligauerat, subfossus ab eadem bestia post
dies muneris obiit; Saturus solummodo tractus est. 6. Et cum
ad ursum substrictus esset in ponte, ursus de cauea prodire
noluit. Itaque secundo Saturus inlaesus reuocatur.

20. Puellis autem ferocissimam uaccam ideoque praeter
consuetudinem conparatam diabolus praeparauit, sexui
earum etiam de bestia aemulatus. 2. Itaque dispoliatae et
reticulis indutae producebantur. Horruit populus alteram
respiciens puellam delicatam, alteram a partu recentem
stillantibus mammis. 3. Ita reuocatae et discinctis indutae.
Prior Perpetua iactata est et concidit in lumbos. 4. Et ubi
sedit, tunicam a latere discissam ad uelamentum femoris
reduxit pudoris potius memor quam doloris. 5. Dehinc acu
requisita et dispersos capillos infibulauit; non enim decebat
martyram sparsis capillis pati, ne in sua gloria plangere
uideretur. 6. Ita surrexit et elisam Felicitatem cum uidisset,
accessit et manum ei tradidit et suscitauit illam. Et ambae
pariter steterunt. 7. Et populi duritia deuicta, reuocatae sunt
in portam Sanauiuariam. 8. Illic Perpetua a quodam tunc
catechumeno Rustico nomine qui ei adhaerebat, suscepta et
quasi a somno expergita (adeo in spiritu et in extasi fuerat)
circumspicere coepit et stupentibus omnibus ait:

Quando, inquit, producimur ad uaccam illam nescio-
quam?

9. Et cum audisset quod iam euenerat, non prius cred-
idit nisi quasdam notas uexationis in corpore et habitu suo
recognouisset. 10. Exinde accersitum fratrem suum et illum
catechumenum, adlocuta est dicens:

In fide state et inuicem omnes diligite, et passionibus
nostris ne scandalizemini.

21. Item Saturus in alia porta Pudentem militem exhortabatur dicens:

Ad summam, inquit, certe, sicut praesumpsi et praedixi, nullam usque adhuc bestiam sensi. Et nunc de toto corde credas: ecce prodeo illo, et ab uno morsu leopardi consummor.

2. Et statim in fine spectaculi leopardo obiectus de uno morsu tanto perfusus est sanguine, ut populus revertenti illi secundi baptismatis testimonium reclamauerit:

Saluum lotum! Saluum lotum!

3. Plane utique saluus erat qui hoc modo lauerat. 4. Tunc Pudenti militi, [inquit]

Vale, inquit, et memento fidei et mei: et haec te non conturbent, sed confirment.

5. Simulque ansulam de digito eius petiit, et uulneri suo mersam reddidit ei hereditatem, pignus relinquens illi et memoriam sanguinis. 6. Exinde iam exanimis prosternitur cum ceteris ad iugulationem solito loco. 7. Et cum populus illos in medio postularet, ut gladio penetranti in eorum corpore oculos suos comites homicidii adiungerent, ultro surrexerunt et se quo uolebat populus transtulerunt, ante iam osculati inuicem, ut martyrium per sollemnia pacis consummarent. 8. Ceteri quidem inmobiles et cum silentio ferrum receperunt: multo magis Saturus, qui et prior ascenderat, prior reddidit spiritum; nam et Perpetuam sustinebat. 9. Perpetua autem, ut aliquid doloris gustaret, inter ossa conpuncta exululauit, et errantem dexteram tirunculi gladiatoris ipsa in iugulum suum transtulit. 10. Fortasse tanta femina aliter non potuisset occidi, quae ab inmundo spiritu timebatur, nisi ipsa uoluisset. 11. O fortissimi ac beatissimi martyres! O uere uocati et electi in gloriam domini nostri Iesu Christi! Quam qui magnificat et honorificat et adorat,

utique et haec non minora ueteribus exempla in aedificationem Ecclesiae legere debet, ut nouae quoque uirtutes unum
et eundem semper Spiritum Sanctum usque adhuc operari
testificentur, et omnipotentem Deum Patrem et Filium
eius Iesum Christum dominum nostrum, cui est claritas et
inmensa potestas in saecula saeculorum. Amen.

Appendix II: The Acts of the Scillitan Martyrs (English and Latin)

■

English translation

1. When Praesens was consul for the second time and Claudianus for the first, on July seventeenth in Carthage, Speratus, Nartzalus, Cittinus, Donata, Secunda, and Vestia were brought to the governor's office for their hearing. And the governor Saturninus said to them:

"You can earn the pardon of our lord the emperor, if you just come back to your senses."

2. Speratus said:

"We have never done anything wrong. We have never given ourselves to evil-doing. We have never uttered a curse. If fact, when we have been mistreated, we have given thanks, since we honor our emperor."

3. The governor Saturninus said:

"We, too, are religious, and our religion is simple: we swear by the *genius* of our lord the emperor, and we pray for his well-being. And that is what you should do as well."

4. Speratus said:

"If you will listen with an open mind, I can tell you a mystery of simplicity."

5. Saturninus said:

"I will not listen to you denigrating our rites. Instead, you need to swear by the *genius* of our lord the emperor."

6. Speratus said:

"I do not acknowledge an empire of this world. But, rather, I serve that God whom no one sees or is able to see with these eyes. I have not stolen anything, but I pay the taxes on anything I buy, since I acknowledge my Lord, the emperor of kings and of all peoples."

7. Saturninus the governor said to the others:

"Abandon this conviction!"

Speratus said:

"It is a bad conviction to commit murder, to bear false witness."

8. Saturninus the governor said:

"Do not take part in this insanity!"

Cittinus said:

"The only one we fear is our Lord God who is in heaven!"

9. Donata said:

"We render honor to Caesar as Caesar. But we render fear only to God."

Vestia said:

"I am a Christian."

Secunda said:

"I am precisely what I wish to be."

10. Saturninus the governor said to Speratus:

"Do you continue to be a Christian?"

Speratus said:

"I am a Christian."

And they all agreed with him.

11. Saturninus the governor said to them all:

"Don't you want some time to think this over?"

Speratus responded:

"In a matter so just, there is nothing to think over."

12. Saturninus the governor said:

"What do you have there in your bag?"

Speratus said:

"The books and letters of Paul, a just man."

13. Satuninus the governor said:

"Take a thirty day reprieve to think things over."

Speratus said again:

"I am a Christian."

And they all agreed with him.

14. Saturninus the governor read his decision from a tablet:

"Speratus, Nartzalus, Cittinus, Donata, Vestia, Secunda, and others have confessed that they live according to Christian rites; although they have been given the opportunity to return to the Roman way, they have obstinately persevered; I have therefore decided that they are to be executed by the sword."

15. Speratus said:

"We give thanks to God!"

Nartzalus said:

"Today, we are martyrs in heaven. Thanks be to God!"

16. The governor Saturninus ordered that a herald proclaim the following:

"I have ordered the execution of Speratus, Nartzalus, Cittinus, Veturius, Felix, Aquilinus, Laetantius, Januaria, Generosa, Vestia, Donata, and Secunda."

17. They all said together:

"Thanks be to God."

And at once they were beheaded for the name of Christ. Amen.

Latin text

1. Praesente bis et Claudiano consulibus, XVI kalendas augustas, Kartagine in secretario inpositis Sperato, Nartzalo et Cittino, Donata, Secunda, Vestia, Saturninus proconsul dixit:

Potestis indulgentiam domni nostri imperatoris promereri, si ad bonam mentem redeatis.

2. Speratus dixit:

Numquam malefecimus, iniquitati nullam operam praebuimus: numquam malediximus, sed male accepti gratias egimus propter quod imperatorem nostrum obseruamus.

3. Saturninus proconsul dixit:

Et nos religiosi sumus et simplex est religio nostra, et iuramus per genium domni nostri imperatoris et pro salute eius supplicamus, quod et uos quoque facere debetis.

4. Speratus dixit:

Si tranquillas praebueris aures tuas, dico mysterium simplicitatis.

5. Saturninus dixit:

Initianti tibi mala de sacris nostris aures non praebebo; sed potius iura per genium domni nostri imperatoris.

6. Speratus dixit:

Ego imperium huius seculi non cognosco; sed magis illi Deo seruio quem nemo hominum uidit nec uidere his oculis potest. Furtum non feci, sed siquid emero teloneum reddo quia cognosco domnum meum, imperatorem regum et omnium gentium.

7. Saturninus proconsul dixit ceteris:

Desinite huius esse persuasionis.

Speratus dixit:

Mala est persuasio homicidium facere, falsum testimonium dicere.

8. Saturninus proconsul dixit:

Nolite huius dementiae esse participes.

Cittinus dixit:

Nos non habemus alium quem timeamus nisi domnum Deum nostrum qui est in caelis.

9. Donata dixit:

Honorem Caesari quasi Caesari; timorem autem Deo.

Vestia dixit:

Christiana sum.

Secunda dixit:

Quod sum, ipsud uolo esse.

10. Saturninus proconsul Sperato dixit:

Perseueras Christianus?

Speratus dixit:

Christianus sum:

et cum eo omnes consenserunt.

11. Saturninus proconsul dixit:

Numquid ad deliberandum spatium uultis?

Speratus dixit:

In re tam iusta nulla est deliberatio.

12. Saturninus proconsul dixit:

Quae sunt res capsa uestra?

Speratus dixit:

Libri et epistulae Pauli uiri iusti.

13. Saturninus proconsul dixit:

Moram XXX dierum habete et recordemini.

Speratus iterum dixit:

Christianus sum: et cum eo omnes consenserunt.

14. Saturninus proconsul decretum ex tabella recitauit:

Speratum, Nartzalum, Cittinum, Donatam, Vestiam,

Secundam, et ceteros ritu Christiano se uiuere confessos, quoniam oblata sibi facultate ad Romanorum morem redeundi obstinanter perseuerauerunt, gladio animaduerti placet.

15. Speratus dixit:

Deo gratias agimus.

Nartzalus dixit:

Hodie martyres in caelis sumus. Deo gratias.

16. Saturninus proconsul per praeconem dici iussit:

Speratum, Naartzalum, Cittinum, Veturium, Felicem, Aquilinum, Laetantium, Ianuariam, Generosam, Vestiam, Donatam, Secundam duci iussi.

17. Uniuersi dixerunt:

Deo gratias.

Et statim decollati sunt pro nomine Christi. amen.

Appendix III: Chart of the Martyrs' Deaths

None of the ancient authors of <u>Perpetua's Passion</u> thought it important to distinguish in a clear narrative the different sufferings and deaths of martyrs, even though they did not all die at the same time, in the same place, and in the same way. The result is that it can be difficult to keep track of who and how many the Carthaginian martyrs were and of when and how they died. The chart on the following page should assist readers in mapping out the sequence of events and the logistics of the different martyrs' experiences.

Name of Martyr/ Victim	Order/Time of Death	Preliminary Injuries Sustained	Method of Killing Implemented	Place of Death	Section # of Death
Quintus	First	—	—	In jail	11
Jucundus, Saturninus, Artaxius	Second	—	Burnt alive	In the arena	11
Secundulus	Third	—	By the sword	In jail	14
"Venator"	Several days after Geta's contest	Gored by wild boar's tusks (19)	Slow death, result of injuries sustained	—	19
Saturninus, Revocatus	Fourth	Mauled by leopard and bear in stocks (19)	By the sword, publicly	In the arena	21
Saturus	Fifth	Dragged by wild boar (19)	By the sword, publicly	In the arena	21
Rusticus	Sixth	—	By the sword, publicly	In the arena	21
Felicitas	Seventh	Crushed by heifer (20)	By the sword, publicly	In the arena	21
Perpetua	Eighth	Attacked by heifer (20), struck by sword on collarbone (21)	By the sword, publicly	In the arena	21

Appendix IV:
Poems on Martyrdom

■

Early in 2003, the Benedictine Sisters of Baltimore invited the four poets included here – Christine Higgins, Ann LoLordo, Madeleine Mysko, and Kathleen O'Toole – to present a reading at Emmanuel Monastery. When the poets met at the monastery to reflect and plan, they noted that the event would take place on March 7, Feast Day of Saints Perpetua and Felicity. Thus, the ancient story of Perpetua and Felicity became the theme for that reading at the monastery, as each poet responded with a singular poem. Meanwhile, on the Loyola campus, Diana Samet invited the same poets to read for her graphic arts students. Those students designed posters for the texts of the poems, thereby further enriching the response to the ancient story of these two women saints, Perpetua and Felicity.

The Naming
by Christine Higgins

In a dream Perpetua beheld a bronze ladder
with swords and spears entwined around the sides,
ready to snare her if she dared not to look up.
It was the dream of a martyr, ecstatic to be dying
for her beliefs, a woman, barely a woman,
who challenged her father with the word, *Christian.*

On Halloween, when I was eight, and we were
charged by the nuns to dress as our patron saint,
my mother informed me I was named after Christ.
How that disappointed me. I wanted to dress
as St. Elizabeth in a blue veil with a bread basket of roses,
or blind St. Cecilia with eyeballs served up on a silver platter.

How to be like Christ?
A woman who is my patient says: My son is dead,
but before he died, I got to bathe him
head to toe, even his privates, and we weren't ashamed.

If I were climbing a ladder to heaven
entwined in those rungs would be
all manner of things I attend to
instead of keeping an eye on my ascent:
my daughter in her eyelet dress, my silk scarves, my TV set.
Disciples of Buddha say if you do not meditate
about death in the morning, you have wasted your morning.
St Ignatius asks: Do you prefer life over death?

At times, I still dislike my name – *Christine,*
as if I am to be held more accountable than others.
Remember Peter who denied three times?
I'm not brave like Perpetua. I don't want
the whole damn empire to know
I am anointed, marked with the sign of faith.

Redemption
by Christine Higgins

This is a woman's hope:
to put aside her shame
and kneel before him
with precious oil,
prepared to wash his feet,
believing desire alone
is enough to be redeemed.

This is a woman's love:
washing and folding garments,
worrying if there is enough wine,
sweeping the house clean,
placing flowers at the grave.
Caretakers even of the dead.

This is a woman's faith:
to arrive at the tomb
with spices, not knowing
if she will be strong enough
to roll away the stone, but
knowing the thing to do is try.

Perpetua
by Ann LoLordo

The ladder held all manner of things,
spears and hooks and knives,
but I was not deterred,
not by the serpent's tooth or its venom,
for I knew beyond lay my welcome.

A garden with all manner of fruit
and flora, passion fruit and pomegranates,
prickly pears and plums, the dark red center
of my heart. My father had hoped I would renounce
my faith and be freed from the prison
at Carthage, to leave the arena unscathed,
for the sake of my son. But this is the beginning
of my flowering, to rise up and embrace
language, which will free me
from earth's fever and its dark red scent.
Even now, as they oil my body, I am anxious
to be done with all manner of the body,
for though it is comely, it is no longer mine
to give. Felicity and I go together
to take up the bough of golden apples
and leave our children, a son and a daughter,
to retell the story I write today, in my own words.

Felicity, pin up your hair, gather your robe,
kiss me well, the Gate of Life is opening.

Felicity
By Ann LoLordo

What choice do I have, a hand maiden
to a gentle woman who renounces this life?

Rounded up with the others, I follow,
follow her, carrying a gourd of water
to quench her thirst in this dark underground.
The smell of fear trails the men like chained slaves.
I pass a golden ladder ascending into a halo of light,
knowing all manner of beast awaits:
jeweled-eyed leopards, horned cows,
razor-backed boars and prancing bears.
Egyptians stand idly by, cleaning the swords
of purple-robed warriors who return from the arena.
Angels hover behind rose trees, curious
about my daughter, who has not yet entered the light.
I pray for all manner of release, for the will
to free my body of the flesh of my flesh. Delivered,

I reach for my lady's hand and my desire.
I know only to follow. The Gate of Life is open

Women Saints
by Madeleine Mysko

Perpetua, Felicity –
saints with pretty names.
Names that did not come up
when I was running down the alley
with my best and bossy friend Suzanne.

Suzanne – tomboy, also good Catholic girl, child
of a convert – had read *The Lives of the Saints.*
Her favorite game was something she made up,
involving bad people chasing good Christians
and tying them to a tree with a jump rope.
There were no women saints in this game.

It would be just the two of us.
Suzanne had to be the winner –
the Christian, of course – even though
it meant handing over the rope, even though
she was the better runner, and in her heart
would have preferred never to be caught.

At some point, she'd pretend to trip and fall,
assume a saintly posture, and wait for me
to catch up and play the heathen with a passion
to match hers. She waited in vain.

For I was reluctant with that martyr stuff.
I loved Suzanne fiercely, and wanted
to please her, but in my heart preferred to play
baby dolls with my sister and Ruthie Fritz.
The game always fizzled out.
Suzanne would get in a huff and go on home.
I don't think I ever tied her up.

Perpetua. Felicity.
Saints with pretty names that now come up.
And still I'm reluctant with that martyr stuff.
I love the sisterliness of these women,
the moment in the awful arena with the wild beasts
when Perpetua, wounded herself, reaches
a hand to pull Felicity up.

The account leaves me breathless, the heart
beneath my breasts pounding. When her father
begs her to recant, I want to cry *Perpetua!*
It's not too late – not for you, not
for your dear slave Felicity.
Jesus died. Isn't that sacrifice enough?

Perpetua, Perpetua, fly away home.
Your baby is crying, your milk letting down.
It's late in the day. Can you not hear? –
all the children of the world, running
up the alley, hungry for their suppers,
all the children calling *fly away, fly*
away home. Our hearts are on fire, *Perpetua,*
knowing how the story ends, knowing
already the mother has flown.

Lives of the Saints
by Kathleen O'Toole

We children chimed in as the touchstone
names rang out – *Agatha and Lucy,*
Agnes and Cecilia, Perpetua and Felicity –
hypnotized by the timbre if not yet
the tales of these women – *all ye holy virgins*
and martyrs. A tide of syllables like algae
in opaque waves of faith – breakers
shaping the shore.

Only now the urge
to forge new icons. Felicity the maidservant
in sunflower cloth, quiet grace of the Ogoni
woman navigating crowded roadsides
balancing a giant yam in a basket on her head.
The arc of fabric from her raised arm
swaddles her belly. Just a hint of the child to be
softens her stride, the blaze of her eyes.
Perpetua in jade robes and Igbo headcloth
takes her seat in the dusty shadows
to nurse the son born in captivity, brought
to her daily, against her father's will.
A shaft of light from a single window
illuminates the heavy folds of cloth, smooth
skin of a noblewoman's hands, her steady
gaze and brazen hosannas.

One last image
framed in the instant the names *Perpetua*
and Felicity are joined, before a wild cow and
jeering crowds we do not see. Just two women,
arms entwined as if lifting to us
their truth: in love a leveling.

We do not name their companions. The story
once rivaled the gospels as Christian currency –
their courage, their kiss before death,
the white robes radiant, bloodless.

Biographies of the Poets

Christine Higgins – Christine Higgins taught at Loyola College for ten years. She is a poet and non-fiction writer. She is currently at work on a book which chronicles her most recent experience as a counselor at a drug treatment center where she still works part-time. She teaches at Johns Hopkins University in the Master of Writing Graduate Program.

'The Naming' first appeared in the magazine, *America*, in May 2005.

Ann LoLordo – Ann, an editorial writer and editor at The Baltimore Sun, is a graduate of Georgetown University who holds a master's degree from the Johns Hopkins Writing Seminars program. Her poems have appeared in The Greensboro Review, Puerto del Sol and other literary journals. She lives in Crownsville, Md. with her husband and son.

Madeleine Mysko – Madeleine's work, both poetry and prose, has appeared in *The Hudson Review, Shenandoah, River Styx,* and *Smartish Pace* among other journals. Presently she is employed as a registered nurse in a Baltimore retirement community. A graduate of The Writing Seminars of The Johns Hopkins University, she also teaches writing in the Hopkins Odyssey Program.

Kathleen O'Toole – Kathleen has combined a twenty-five year career in community organizing with writing and teaching. She is a 1991 graduate of the Johns Hopkins Writing Seminars. She has taught writing at JHU and the Maryland Institute College of Art. Her chapbook <u>Practice</u>

was published this year by Finishing Line Press, and individual poems have appeared in *Poetry, AMERICA, The Notre Dame Review, Natural Bridge and The Ledge,* among others. She currently works at Bread for the World and lives in Takoma Park, MD with her husband John Ruthrauff.

'Lives of the Saints' first appeared in *Notre Dame Review*, in January 2006.

apprentice
house

Apprentice House is the future of publishing...today. Using state-of-the-art technology and an experiential learning model of education, it publishes books in untraditional ways while teaching tomorrow's future editors and publishers.

Staffed by students, this non-profit activity of the Department of Communication at Loyola College in Maryland is part of an advanced elective course and overseen by the press's Director. When class is not in session, work on book projects is carried forward by a co-curricular organization, The Apprentice House Book Publishing Club, of which the press's Director also serves as Faculty Advisor.

Contributions are welcomed to sustain the press's work and are tax deductible to the fullest extent allowed by the IRS. For more information, see www.apprenticehouse.com.

Student Editors (2005-06)

Jerrell Cameron

Meghan Connolly

Katharine Dailey

Kinzee Ellis

Natalie Joseph

Dana Kirkpatrick

Ann Marshall

Joanna Walsh

Alison Wright

Kevin Zazzali

CPSIA information can be obtained at www.ICGtesting.com
Printed in the USA
BVOW02s1129150913

331207BV00001B/11/A